YO-AAX-153

Jerry Stefaniak's new relationship book is a welcome resource for couples who want practical, down-to-earth tools for achieving what is one of the most difficult goals to attain in life: a healthy love relationship. Jerry tells it like it is and we believe him because he convinces us he has been there. Some of the personal relationship breakdowns he shares are downright comedic, (and certainly will evoke in most of us our own relational boondoggles). And sometimes after loosening us up with his disarmingly honest revelations, he hits us between the eyes with the solution, often something as profound in its simplicity as it is in its effectiveness. Many of the challenges and issues commonly experienced in relationships are addressed with creativity and optimism. And with the book's evident spiritual grounding, based on *A Course in Miracles*, Jerry operates from the important premise that couples, first of all, need a spiritual foundation. As a member of a psychotherapist couple myself, and working with lots of couples, I see Jerry's book as a great, easy-to-read relationship companion, and one I will recommend to my clients.

**Jerry Goodman LMSW-ACP**

Jerry, thank you for a book that presents *A Course in Miracles* relationship principles in easily understood conversational language. I love how you share your personal experience of your spiritual journey into relationships. Thank you also for the practical tools you provide in helping me to better my relationships.

**Janice Gabriels**

This is a very strong book. The author provides information and devices for introspection and self-discovery that really stand on their own. The author is an experienced relationship advisor and workshop leader and his information is valuable, authoritative, and well written. Rev. Stefaniak has created a well-written, easy-to-read, engaging book.

**Book reviewer for Llewellyn Publishers**

I think the Reverend Stefaniak is on to something unique and effective, with his use of humor to reinforce valid points, and, not so incidentally, to relieve stress.

**Bunny Hoest, Syndicated Cartoonist**

No matter what kind of relationship you have right now, there's something in this book that you can use. Every relationship—whether friend, partner, husband or wife—can use a good dose of "*Intimacy in Action*"!

**Phaedra Rogers**

In *Intimacy in Action - Relationships that Feed the Soul* Rev. Stefaniak continues what he began with Compassionate Living, a sharing of his knowledge and personal experiences on the path of personal growth. His message that life and relationships are about growing, healing, loving and joy is delivered with humor, insight and, of course, compassion. His conversational style makes for easy reading as he coaxes, prods, reassures, and loves us into creating the life and relationships we truly want.

**Carol Stein**

In *Intimacy in Action - Relationships that Feed the Soul*, Jerry Stefaniak offers the reader a new experience of forgiveness of him/herself and others. Inspired by *A Course in Miracles*, he masterfully blends spiritual principles into the everyday challenges of relationships. His own love of God and his appreciation of our humanness permeates his writing. This is a book that will help open your heart, and thus, receive the relationships of your dreams.

**Coky Gray**

1/28/03

Dear Christina & Gary,

May your Intimacy
(Love, caring, sharing, hopes, dreams etc.)
grow through your actions.

We Love You!
always,   :) xxoo
Mom & Dad

# Intimacy In Action
## *Relationships That Feed The Soul*

# Intimacy in Action

*Relationships That Feed the Soul*

by
Rev. Jerome Stefaniak
*with Stav Stefaniak, MSW, LMSW-ACP*

## Inner Awakenings

Houston, Texas

This book is based on many of the concepts taught in *A Course in Miracles*® and my personal trainings as well as my experience of life and God. The ideas expressed within are **my interpretation** of the concepts of the *Course* and are not endorsed by the copyright holder of *A Course in Miracles*®.

*A Course in Miracles*® was retypeset in 1992 which included the numbering of all sections, paragraphs and sentences. The quotes I use from the *Course* are identified by the page number from the first edition and then the second edition respectively.

Portions of *A Course in Miracles*® copyright 1975, 1992, reprinted by permission of the Foundation for *A Course in Miracles*®

In some cases the names of the people mentioned in anecdotes in this book have been changed. In other cases, I used real names. Which are real and which have been changed will be kept in my heart.

Printed in the United States of America
Cover design by Schmidt & Kay Productions
Original text layout by Jerry Stefaniak
Final layout for production by Brockton Publishing Company

ISBN 1-887918-39-6

*Printed in cooperation with Brockton Publishing Company, Houston, Texas.*
*www.brocktonpublishing.com*
*800-968-7065*

Copyright © June 2000 by Jerome Stefaniak. All rights reserved.
No part of this book may be reproduced without the written permission of the author.
For information, write:

**Rev. Jerome Stefaniak**

11306 Overbrook

Houston, TX 77077

# Acknowledgments

Many people had a hand in creating this book. Actually, every person I ever met did their part in shaping and teaching me. Sometimes it took many years before I learned why I attracted certain people and events in my life. And of course, every relationship I had did her part in teaching me the meaning of love and life.

Also along the way, I was blessed to meet some wonderful teachers who really accelerated my learning. I thank Joe and Sandra Heaney for starting me on the path of healing with their Six Month Program and Practitioner Training; and Phil and Lura Smedstad who continued my growth in Houston. These four people have been powerful spiritual teachers in my life. They helped me to become conscious of who I really am, the part I play in my world, and the part others play in my world. And, most importantly, they taught me how to laugh along the way.

I thank my parents for the love and support they have given me through the years. They are a good example in teaching me that learning never stops and that we are never too old to grow and change. I consider myself extremely lucky to have parents who are so progressive in their thinking and ahead of their time. I thank my father, Joseph, for instilling in me a sense of humor, acceptance and joy. I thank my mother, Jean, for teaching me independence, a love of music, art, and opening to my creativity.

I also thank the following people whose editing, suggestions and support allowed this book to reach fruition:

- ♦ Joy Togesen
- ♦ Coky Gray
- ♦ Phaedra Rogers
- ♦ Carol Stein
- ♦ Janice Gabriels
- ♦ Connie Schmidt
- ♦ Ron Kaye
- ♦ Jerry Goodman
- ♦ Gerald Oncken, PhD
- ♦ Brocky Brown of Brockton Publishing
- ♦ The Foundation for *A Course in Miracles*.

Also, half of the credit for this book goes to my most personal teacher, lover, friend, and informal book editor—my wife—Stav. Through her editing, suggestions, re-editing and more suggestions, she has made this book into a truly helpful and enjoyable text. For me, Stav is a constant inspiration of intimacy in action. She is a wonderful coach, lover, business partner and fellow adventurer as we teach and practice everything taught in this book.

*Thank you all*

# Contents

## Introduction

## RELATIONSHIP BASICS

## THE LAWS OF RELATIONSHIPS

# FOUNDATIONS OF A CONSCIOUS RELATIONSHIP

# Using All This Stuff

# Introduction

I have had many relationships. Or rather, I should say, I have used many relationships. I have used relationships to help me feel sexually attractive, financially secure, emotionally successful or to just stave off the feelings of loneliness. Like everybody I knew, I got into relationships *not knowing* what I was doing, *not knowing why* I was doing it, but *doing it anyway* because— well, everybody else was doing it and so, that was the thing to do. Nobody modeled a better way. We were similar to lemmings running off a cliff!

But there came a time, in every one of those relationships, that I would ask myself, "Is that all there is?"

Something was missing.

Mother Theresa once said, "America is rich materially, but impoverished spiritually."

This book is about increasing the intimacy with ourselves and others. It's about opening to the idea that loving, fulfilling relationships are not only possible, but also our right. It's about learning to feed and nurture the emotional and spiritual side of our relationships—it's about feeding and nurturing our souls. More and more people are beginning to realize that our lives, relationships, and prosperity are anchored in something deeper than just the material world we see. After years of striving for that golden career, the perfect relationship, or financial security, we find our souls empty, still longing for something more, still spiritually hungry. Joseph Campbell said it best: "Many men spend their lives climbing the ladder of success only to find that it's been resting against the wrong wall."

I have spent many years climbing the ladder of relationships, only to be disappointed and find that my ladder was resting on the wrong wall. I based my relationships on money, sex, career, or companionship, only to find the final goal empty and unrewarding. I didn't know it, but I was starving for something more. And no woman, job, car, or house could ever sufficiently nourish the aching hunger inside of me. After many years of searching *out there* for the answer I finally embarked upon a journey of self-discovery. Initially I saw a scared, seemingly flawed child—one that was full of defenses and embedded in unconscious reactivity.

But as I peeled away the layers of negativity, guilt and self-hatred, I found the answers had been within me all the time. I took classes and learned how to become more honest, conscious and intentional with myself and my relationships. I learned how to communicate effectively and to take responsibility for how my life looked.

And a wonderful thing began to happen. As I worked on myself, my relationships seemed to improve, and, as I worked on improving my relationships, I found that I loved myself more. It was like a wonderful circle in which no matter what I did, I got better. Ultimately I rediscovered the precious child within.

This book is the result of years of trial and error, drawing on the tools and knowledge that help Stav (my wife) and me to have the kind of loving relationship that not only empowers ourselves and each other, but also the world. This book draws on both psychological and spiritual principles. The psychological concepts are from the years of training that we have given and received, from our personal experiences and from working with our clients.

Many of the spiritual concepts in this book are from *A Course in Miracles*. I have found these books to be a powerful teacher in helping me to see my world through new eyes. They have helped me to see relationships differently and to give me hope that yes, indeed, people really can have relationships that work!

If you are new to *A Course in Miracles,* you may find some of the metaphysical and spiritual concepts upsetting, alarming or even downright scary. I know I felt that way initially. But once I got past my initial resistance to changing my mind about myself, others and God, I began to see that these books were actually designed to lead me back into sanity, happiness and wholeness.

Though it may seem that I am focusing on committed, heterosexual relationships, it is important to know that the concepts in this book are applicable to **all types** of relationships. The basis of true, loving relationships has nothing to do with marriage, gender, sexual preference, skin color or religion. A relationship is the *interaction* and healing between two people, not how the relationship *looks* to the world. A loving, dynamic relationship is the experience of connection between two souls. It is *intimacy in action*.

Stav and I have been married for over 35 years—the last eleven years to each other. We do not discount our past relationships. We do not pretend they never happened. We do not ignore the hurts and experiences that led us to the relationship we currently have. We use everything we've learned as building blocks to better our lives. The saying, "Those who do not learn from history are doomed to repeat it," is especially true in relationships. My wife and I use our histories not to hold onto old grudges or perpetuate being right about men or women, but to learn from them, to see what we did wrong and to change our present relationship.

This book was written to share with you our pilgrimage and to hopefully help you to open up to the love and gifts of the people in your life. But more importantly, I hope it helps you to open up to love yourself. This book is a *guide* and a roadmap to saner, more loving relationships. If you find sections in this book that bring up anger or defensiveness, do not fight the feelings. Notice them and then continue—or put the book down until you are ready to try again. Fifteen years ago many of the thoughts and ideas that I now teach I originally thought were downright stupid, too optimistic or airy-fairy. But the seeds were planted, and, after years of doing it *my way* and seeing that it didn't produce the results I wanted, I thought,

"What the hell! Let's try out those ideas!"

As I experimented with these techniques, as I tried seeing my relationships differently, as I experienced my relationships in a new way, I found that these ideas indeed changed my life for the better.

The questions or affirmations at the end of each chapter are designed to help you to try on new ideas and to shake up your perceptions—to help you get new insights about yourself. There are four parts to this book. They are: **Relationship Basics, The Laws of Relationships, The Foundations of a Conscious Relationship** and, finally, **Using All This Stuff.**

Do not feel as if you have to read this book in the order it is presented. This book is meant to help the reader with any issue they may be having and so, feel free to skip to the chapters that immediately interest you. The first section, **Relationship Basics,** explains the ***What*** of relationships, the purpose, goal setting and how relationships generally evolve. It covers a lot of the metaphysical and spiritual aspects of relationships. The second section, **The Laws of Relationships** explains the ***Why*** of relationships—why relationships are the way they are. The last two sections, **Foundations of a Conscious Relationship** and **Using All This Stuff** explain the ***How*** of relationships.

If you are having an argument with your partner right now, you can turn to the chapter entitled **Getting Back to the Love** for immediate help. Later you can read the preceding sections for more clarification. If you are new to the concept that our thoughts create, and you want to know how to change your old thoughts through the use of affirmations, go to the last chapter, **How to Use Affirmations,** to learn how to use this powerful tool.

This book in no way covers every aspect of relationships and is not meant to. I wanted to share with you the tools that Stav and I have used to empower our relationship, and the principles we teach to the many people who attend our workshops, classes and talks. Through the years, we have been constantly surprised at the wonderful lessons that are presented, the old thoughts that still need to be healed, and finally seeing our partner's side of an issue. But most importantly we have been most happily surprised at the love that pops up when these tools are used. We have learned to laugh—at ourselves, the world, even God. God is the Father of joy and He loves it when we enjoy His creations. Let this book be a step into creating joy in your relationships and in your soul. Let your life be filled with love, life and happiness. When you do, you will create many "Ah-Ha!" and "Ha-Ha!" experiences.

# What Is *A Course in Miracles?*

*A Course in Miracles* is a spiritual text that provides a practical application of spiritual principles in our daily lives. It is a study in learning how to **change our minds**. It's a course on remembering that we are not the victims of a world *out there*, but powerful, loving, creative spirits who can create the reality we think we desire. The *Course* is a path out of our self-created hells. It is an invitation back to our sanity.

*A Course in Miracles* is comprised of three books, a 669-page *Text*; a 488-page *Workbook for Students* which has 365 lessons, one for every day of the year; and a 92-page *Manual for Teachers*.

The *Course* came into my life at a crucial time, a time when my life was all mixed up and I was totally lost and confused. It was a time when I was at my lowest point and doubted everything about myself. The *Course* entered my life and introduced me to some seemingly radical ideas that slowly began to transform my life. With the Course, and a lot of help from friends and teachers, I began to change my mind about the world, love, relationships, God, and finally, myself.

## *How It Came To Be Written*

Helen Schucman scribed *A Course in Miracles* with the help of Bill Thedford. Both of these people were psychologists, professors and co-workers at Columbia University in New York City. There was a lot of fighting and aggressiveness among the staff at the hospital and after one particularly bad incident, Bill remarked to Helen that he was tired of the angry and aggressive feelings their attitudes reflected, and concluded that there *"must be a better way."* His statement struck a chord in her, and Helen immediately agreed to help *find a way*.

Helen was very spiritual, but she had a strong dislike and suspicion of orthodox religions. Though she came from a Jewish background and had contact with other faiths, Helen considered herself an agnostic. Her skepticism followed her throughout her life. While scribing the *Course*, she questioned and challenged what she wrote, many times fighting and arguing with the words that flowed through her. Even after she had finished writing *A Course in Miracles,* she still questioned and doubted herself and her abilities.

Regardless, throughout her life she would experience vivid dreams and visions. Periodically a loving Voice would talk to her. She would relate these dreams and conversations to her husband and to Bill. Her husband found her dreams to be disturbing and advised her to forget about them. But Bill found them interesting, urging her to share them with him. Being a psychologist, not surprisingly, her dreams and visions brought up fears of her own sanity and credibility. And so she decided to ignore the Voice and the visions.

But a few months after their agreement to *"find a better way,"* Helen told Bill that the Voice had returned. She said that the Voice was telling her, *"This is a course in miracles. Please take notes."* Bill advised her to take notes, assuring her that he would keep her confidence, and if it seemed crazy, they could just rip it up. After reading her first transcription, Bill knew that this material was something new and important, and he supported her in continuing. Daily he would type her notes from the night before. And so, over a period of seven and a half years, the *Course* was born. Throughout this time, Helen was vehemently opposed to showing the material to anyone. It took awhile for her to calm her fears and realize that this was a gift that needed to be shared with the world.

The Voice of *A Course in Miracles* makes no secret in letting us know that it is Jesus Christ speaking. At first I disbelieved it. I thought it was just a bunch of hokey, New Age nonsense. In fact, it downright scared me! But as I read more and more of the *Course*, I found myself no longer caring who spoke the words, or how they came to be written. What I felt was a stirring of Truth in my heart. These words felt vaguely familiar and true—like a forgotten memory, trying to resurface.

I found the *Course* aggravating in its persistent acknowledgment of *my* responsibility for the pain in my life, but heartening as it reminded me of my innocence and Divine nature. It also stressed the importance of becoming responsible and aware of my inner-most thoughts and fears, because it was with these thoughts and fears that I was creating my reality. My turning point came in Chapter Six – *The Lessons in Love*, in which Jesus explains the purpose of His crucifixion.

Ever since I was a child, the thought that Jesus *died for my sins* made no sense to me. How could a man, 2,000 years ago somehow pay for my sins today? How could God be so cruel as to sacrifice one of His children to die for others? Why did He have to die for my sins, anyway? Nobody could ever answer these questions to my satisfaction. If you are interested in the answer to these questions, or maybe an answer to your own, read Chapter Six – *The Lessons in Love*.

I feel *A Course in Miracles* is a furthering of the lessons Jesus attempted to teach us while He was on Earth and a deeper explanation of His teachings. According to Him, every person we meet can be our savior because as we see others, we see ourselves. And as we change how we see them, we change our vision of ourselves, which, in turn, changes our world. That is the basis of a sane relationship.

I also feel that it is an opportunity for Jesus to correct some of the misrepresentations of what He originally was trying to say. In the Course He actually corrects some of the statements attributed to Him and reaffirms that His message was always about love and nothing else. He also exposes the reader to a loving God and not the God so many of us have learned to be afraid of.

Although the *Course* emphasizes that it is only one of many paths back to Truth, I have found that *A Course in Miracles* speaks to me more than any other spiritual text that I have read. It has truly restored sanity to my life.

# *What the Course Teaches*
## *(Briefly!)*

One of the basic concepts the *Course* teaches is that we are constantly choosing to live our lives based on either love or fear. When we choose not to confront our partner for their abuse, we are choosing fear. When we decide not to tell our lover the truth about an issue because his/her love may go away or because they may get upset, we are choosing fear. When we hide who we are— our dreams, desires and our goals—because the world may judge us, we are choosing fear.

When we choose fear, we contract, we get small (after all, a smaller target *is* harder to hit). We look at everything we ever did wrong and expect to be punished. We look at the world with guilty, fearful eyes and perceive only fearful images. And since our egos don't want to take responsibility for our own fears, judgements and guilt, we then project our internal insanity out onto the world that *we see*. We begin to blame others for all of our problems. We judge others for the same things that we judge ourselves. And in doing this, we create *our reality*—a reality based on fear, lack, guilt and judgment. A real hell!

On the other hand, when we take a risk and express our truth and our feelings, knowing our partner may get upset and may even leave, we are *facing our fears* and now choosing love. When we face our unconscious prejudices, our doubts and our past mistakes, and correct them, that is choosing love. As the barriers we have erected begin to fall, miracles occur. We feel lighter, we experience more peace and harmony in our lives and in our relationships. We begin to realize that that there was love around us all the time.

A note of warning: If this is the first time that you are being introduced to these concepts, you may be feeling overwhelmed, anxious or even a little angry. I too felt angry and defensive at the thought that I was responsible for my life. But take heart! The rest of this book is devoted to explaining how these ideas work in more bite-sized pieces.

The *Course* emphasizes **application** of spiritual principles rather than theory, **experience** rather than theology. It states,

*A universal theology is impossible, but a universal experience is not only possible but necessary.*
**Teachers Manual pg.** 73 / 77

Where the world would tell us that you can only attain God through a certain religion or ritual, the Course emphasizes that it is everyone's right to *experience* God no matter how they get there. And once one experiences God, the method of getting there no longer matters. A Hindu's experience of God is no different than a Christian's. They may have gotten to that experience through different methods, but they can definitely appreciate, honor and accept the depth of each other's experience, and honor each other's essence.

Where the world would tell us that its perceptions are true, the *Course* says that the world you perceive is the world you *believe* you will perceive. And a miracle is a *change in our perception*. As we change our perceptions of who we think we are, our world miraculously changes with it. Where once there was hate, there is now love. Where once there was pain and revenge, there is now transcendent forgiveness. Where once there was unrelenting fear, now there is unlimited peace.

When I finally faced my fears and judgments about women and began to see them as loving, caring, dynamic people, instead of the secretive, mean, incomprehensible creatures I *thought* they were, that was a miracle! And miraculously my relationships with them have gotten better ever since.

Of course, this miracle did not happen all at once. It was many, many miracles, many mini-changes of my perceptions that, over time, gave me a better understanding of myself and others. Actually, being willing to change your mind about anything is essentially the first miracle.

When we let go of our guilt, we find our lives working more smoothly and with less self-sabotage. When we face our fear and demonstrate the Truth about ourselves, our world begins to change.

When we are willing to see the love in our partner's eyes instead of the hate and judgement we *think* is there, our relationships become more harmonious. When we see with the Vision of Christ, instead of the body's eyes, we see possibilities, we see love, we see heaven. What the *Course* is teaching us is how to have an experience of Heaven *here on earth.* At one point it states,

> *Heaven has come because it found a home in your relationship on earth.*

**Text pg. 424 / 455**

Giving you tools to change your mind, find peace, release your fear, and create miracles—is the goal of this book.

# Relationship Basics

*For many years, I thought I knew what relationships were for and how to have them. The truth is, I had no idea of even the basic fundamentals. Like many others, I suffered because of my ignorance. I drifted from person to person, situation to situation, blaming one after another, or blaming God or blaming myself. But once the pain got severe enough to force me to dig deep within myself, I began to see that there was a conscious and an unconscious purpose to the relationships I had. I began to see my part in the drama and I became aware of the patterns that I never knew existed. And I began to have hope and to see the light at the end of the tunnel of despair.*

*A relationship is the commitment to each other's*
*well being and companionship*
*in the large adventure of life.*

**Stewart Emery,** *Actualizations*


*By all means marry;*
*if you get a good wife, you'll become happy;*
*if you get a bad one, you'll become a philosopher.*

**Socrates**


*A man always has two reasons for doing*
*anything — a good reason and the real reason.*

**John Pierpont Morgan**


*A good relationship is like a shark.*
*It has to keep moving to stay alive.*
*What I think we have here is a dead shark.*

**Woody Allen in** *Annie Hall*


*I have never met a man so ignorant*
*that I couldn't learn something from him.*

**Galileo Galilei**

# The Purpose of Relationships

Have you ever asked yourself why you want a relationship in the first place? The world has many reasons for being in a relationship, such as having sex, babies, security, a cosy house with a white picket fence, someone to cook and clean, someone to create the money, someone to take care of us, someone to keep us from feeling lonely, etc. It's something you're expected to do when you grow up. When people think that these things are what relationships are for, they are bound to be disappointed. While these purposes historically served our parents and grandparents well, people today want more out of a relationship.

In a dynamic, loving relationship, those original purposes are the icing on the cake—not the cake itself. Security, prosperity, companionship and a pretty home are the rewards we receive when we open to our real selves and to the love of another. And, as we open to our real selves, we find it easier and easier to open up to others.

According to *A Course in Miracles*, the purpose of relationships is to heal—to heal the separation we feel between ourselves and others and between ourselves and God. It is also to heal the separation and the sense of isolation we feel within ourselves *with* ourselves. Recent findings also mirror what the *Course* is saying. Harville Hendrix, for example, states that the ultimate purpose of relationships is to repeat and repair childhood wounds. And in repairing our childhood wounds, we become one with our true selves.

By now you may be thinking,

"Relationships are for healing? What fun! Sounds like having to take medicine or vitamins."

Just because relationships are meant to heal does not mean that they can't be fun. In fact, *that is how you know you are healing.* You're having more fun, more play, more sex, more prosperity! You feel fulfilled, energized, loved and nurtured as you yourself fulfill, energize, love and nurture. Healing should not be considered like taking medicine ("I'm doing this because it's *good* for me.") There is a joy and excitement as two people learn about who they are, what they like and how to love. It is an **adventure** into the uncharted territory of our minds, and we no longer have to do it alone. Relationships like these are never boring.

Albert Einstein once said,

"The significant problems we face cannot be solved at the level of thinking that created them."

Relationships heal when they are used for growth. They force us to **raise** our level of thinking to the level that can solve our problems. They push and pull us into new levels of thinking, if we are open to them.

What needs to be healed? Any unresolved childhood wound, any old hurts that still bring us pain, any suspicion that keeps us in fear needs healing. Relationships are the quickest way to revisit those old ghosts and heal the wounds. And as we heal, we find we like ourselves more. It becomes easier for us to be with the world and for the world to be with us.

So, what does healing look like? In short, it is becoming more conscious of our hidden thoughts and emotions. It is dropping our masks and acts. It is not an all-at-once, now-you're-done experience. It is a gradual unraveling of every perception that you have about yourself and others.

Let's suppose you're having an argument. And suddenly you realize that you are angrier than the situation warrants. *That is healing.*

Maybe it occurs to you that the reason you are angrier than the situation warrants is because maybe there is anger at somebody else *included* in this current anger. *That is healing.*

And when you think about it, you realize that there is a lot of unresolved anger toward your parents (or ex-spouse or an old teacher) mixed in with this anger you have with your relationship. *That is healing.*

You see that you are projecting onto your partner not only the anger you have at what they did, but also all the unexpressed anger you have at others from your past. You realize that your partner is getting a double dose of anger. *That is healing.*

And so you take a risk and tell your partner this fact. *That is healing.*

Maybe both of you begin to talk about past hurts, how each of you was affected. *That is healing.*

You may even decide to get counseling, read books or take workshops in order to understand and correct the errors. *That is healing.*

Now, don't think that you have to go out right now and get into a relationship with someone so that you can heal. You are in some form of relationship all of the time. You create relationships with your coworkers, fellow commuters, as you order food in a restaurant, with your children, etc. And each one can teach you a little bit about yourself. You treat the world at large as you treat yourself. As you relate to the world, so too do you relate and think of yourself. If you see others through judging eyes, you also see yourself through those same eyes. The way you treat others is the way you, yourself, *expect* to be treated. As the *Course* states,

> *When you meet anyone, remember it is a holy encounter. As you see him you will see yourself. As you treat him you will treat yourself. As you think of him you will think of yourself. Never forget this, for in him you will find yourself or lose yourself."*
>
> **Text pg. 131 / 142**

In her book, *Building Your Field of Dreams*, Mary Mannin Morrissey tells the story of how one day she was in the line of an ill-mannered checkout lady at a grocery store. The cashier rang up the wrong price for an item and when Mary brought her attention to it, the woman tersely corrected the entry and rudely gave Mary her change. As Mary left the store, she remarked to the boy carrying her groceries how rude the lady had been.

"Yeah," he replied. "She's upset because her child was in an accident yesterday and is now in the hospital. She can't afford to take the day off from work."

Abruptly Mary's perception of the cashier was changed from a snippy, rude person to someone who was hurting and needed love. It was a lesson for Mary to continually be aware that even when others seem to be treating us badly, there is another side to the story, so we must be willing to have a little compassion, even in the face of seeming rudeness.

This is what relationships offer—the opportunity to change our perceptions and to see things differently.

Something that helped me embrace the purpose of relationships was an incident that happened in my Practitioner training, which I took in order to learn how to use Breath Integration and become a spiritual counselor. I had just broken up with my girlfriend and I was sitting in class, depressed and dejected and feeling like a failure. Rev. Phil Smedstad happened to be teaching that day, and he asked me what was wrong. I told him.

"Would you like some support?" he asked.

"Yes."

"OK, Jerry, would you be willing to go through *anything* in order to create your perfect relationship?"

"Yes I would."

"Really?"

"Yeah, I'd do anything."

"REEEEAAAALLLLY? Anything?"

"Well. . . yes. . . . I think I would."

"What if it took you fifty relationships?"

I sat there, stunned, my mind spinning off scenarios. What if it took me fifty relationships to create the partner I always wanted?

What if it took fifty times of getting my heart stomped on, fifty times of hurting others, fifty times feeling this loneliness, fifty times feeling like a failure? What if I went through all that and then got the type of relationship *I always wanted?* Was it worth it to me?

I realized it was.

I looked up, scared and a little unsure.

"Yes," I said, "I would do it — even if it took fifty relationships."

And I felt something inside me shift. I suddenly realized how I considered every relationship that I got into as THE RELATIONSHIP. And I was so afraid to make a mistake. I was so afraid of losing THE RELATIONSHIP, that I would hold back communicating my truth, I would hold back my needs, I would hold back my love. I saw every relationship as a relationship based on what I could *get*, not on what I could *learn*. I was so afraid to change or grow, lest I lose who I thought I had. And I suddenly felt, "Well, what the hell! If I can someday have the relationship I've always wanted, I can take any lessons I need to learn. I'm going to learn as much as I can, even if it takes fifty tries!"

After that, my intention in relationships was, "How much can I learn, about me, about women and about love?" I stopped gauging my success on how long the relationship lasted, and looked at how much I was learning and how much fun I was having. In my training it became a sort of inside joke.

"How are your relationships going, Jerry?"

"Great! Only got 47 more to go!"

When I relaxed around my relationships, I found that I was easier to be with and people enjoyed my company. And not surprisingly, I didn't have to go through fifty relationships; in fact, six months later I was dating Stav, my future wife.

I transformed my view of relationships from what could I get, to what could I heal about myself. I began to ask myself,

"What is it *I do* that pushes love away, and what can I do to magnetize more love into my life?"

This new perception finally stopped *some* of the insanity in my life. When Stav and I decided that love and more fun was the purpose of our relationship, it changed from an ego-centered to a love-centered relationship. We wanted to have a conscious relationship that was based on applying solid principles. It gave us a new goal—a goal that we could actually attain. This set in motion a life-long romance. We have been having fun ever since!

A good relationship is dynamic. That means that it is always shifting, changing and growing. Why are relationships healing? They slowly teach us to drop our own projections and defenses. They heal us because they bring up everything within us that our egos would prefer to hide or forget. But hiding or forgetting an old experience is harmful when you continually live your life using those old hurts to evaluate the world. If I have unhealed pain with my mother and I suppress the memory, I may feel unaware of my issues with my mom, but I will act out those issues in every relationship I have. I will be distrustful and fearful, even though I may not be aware of the reason why, and I will create upsets until I finally face the pain.

Relationships activate old wounds, old hurts, unforgiven grudges, so that ultimately, we may become aware of why we act and react the way we do, why we hate the way we hate, and why we love the way we love. Hopefully, as we become aware of our grudges, hurts, judgments and pain, we begin to realize how holding onto them keeps us in hell, and we begin to have compassion for ourselves (for not knowing any better) and for others (for their not knowing any better.) This process then leads to forgiveness. As we forgive, we begin to see the world through new eyes; we begin to see the love that has been around us **all the time**.

The purpose of healing is to once again return to our right minds, to become "sane" once again—and to experience more fun and joy in our lives. Pain comes from **resisting** the lesson that life is trying to teach us. At our health club, I saw a sign for massage that I think pertains to every aspect of our lives:

"Pain is inevitable. But suffering is optional."

I believe that it is healthy to realize that self-growth and relationships all involve *some* pain. Not because these activities are themselves painful, but because we all have resistance to seeing our part in every aspect of our lives. It's holding onto old grievances and destructive ways of thinking that prolongs our suffering.

What we are ultimately healing is the feeling of separation we feel between ourselves, others and God. Of course, many of us may not be aware of this feeling of separation, but it does show up in our loneliness, in our self-loathing, in the secrets we think we need to hide and in the separation we feel from others. We think we are the only one with our particular problem, and we think that we are the only one who can solve our problems.

Feeling separated from our own selves also makes us feel separate from others and God. It is this inner self-alienation that makes us feel so lonely. It is this alienation that makes us feel as if there is no love great enough to fill the black hole we feel exists in our hearts.

But as we heal our relationship with ourselves, **or**, as we heal our relationship with others, **or**, as we heal our relationship with God (it's all the same thing!), we feel more connected, we experience more peace, we see that we are lovable, that we do deserve love and that, indeed, we are not empty or alone.

# Affirmations

- *My partner is my path back to God.*
- *As I open more to the love within my partner, I open more to God.*
- *Since I am always going back to God, I now use every experience in my life to take me closer to God.*
- *It gets easier and easier for me to heal.*
- *Life is meant to be enjoyed.*
- *It gets easier and easier for me to help others heal.*
- *When others heal, I also heal.*
- *When I heal, the world heals.*
- *I see God as I see my partner.*
- *As I open more to the love within myself, I open more to God.*
- *God is no further than my heart.*
- *Healing is fun!*

*Many a man in love with a dimple
makes the mistake of marrying the whole girl.*
**Stephen Leacock**


*Always do right;
this will gratify some people
and astonish the rest.*
**Mark Twain**


*Many a man has fallen in love with a girl
in a light so dim
he would not have chosen a suit by it.*
**Maurice Chevalier**


*Love is not gazing longingly into each other's
eyes, but gazing outward in the same direction.*
**Antoine de Expurney**

# You Can Have
# a Holy Relationship –
# or Holy Hell

A *Course in Miracles* states that there are two types of relationships: **special relationships**, which are based on fear, and **holy relationships**, which are based on love. A special relationship is what most of us have experienced in this world. It is a relationship based on outward appearance and the concept of need/obligate. I *need* you in order to feel good about myself, and I will do anything to make you feel *obligated* to stay with me. A special relationship is based on a basic thought that "I am incomplete" and therefore I need to find somebody to complete me. In the terminology of current thinking, a special relationship is *codependent.*

Any tool that can keep this relationship going, such as guilt, fear, self-sacrifice, is fair game. Many of us are familiar with the self-sacrificing, martyr mom who uses guilt to keep her children under her thumb. Other tools that are commonly used are: sexual manipulation, illness, addiction, alcoholism, or financial dependency. Some of us use sex in order to control. Those in recovery are familiar with the drama that comes from alcoholism and addictions. Maybe when we were children, the only time we received love and attention was when we were sick, and so we learn to rely on illness to get the attention we want. Or we may use financial dependency: "I can't live without you because I have no job skills and you are therefore responsible for my life." Many of us have a basic fear of abandonment, and when the thought of loneliness threatens, we bring out every weapon that can be used in order to keep our partner in line.

Meeting a specific form, or outward appearance, plays a big part in the special relationship. Since we think that our partner is meant to fulfill certain needs, our partner must also fit a certain form. And if the form changes, the relationship is threatened. For example, a relationship based on money is threatened when the money runs out, or a relationship based on youthful looks ends when wrinkles begin to appear. When partners get into a relationship to *get something* from the other, there is an undercurrent of guilt and fear. The guilt is because we know, deep inside, that the only reason we are with this person is because she is pretty, or he is rich, and if circumstances change, we may not stay. There is also fear because we are afraid that if our partner leaves, he or she will take away that part we believe completes us.

The relationships our parents and grandparents had were very different from the relationships that we try to create. Relationships in the past were designed to fulfill a function: to start a family, to have a partner to help build a lifestyle or business, and to somehow survive together. In the past we were told, "Stay together no matter what and someday, maybe you'll love each other." But, nowadays, we expect more from our partners. Not only does he or she have to look nice and have a decent job to provide for a future, but also we want our partner to be our mentor, our friend, our perfect sex partner and our counselor. As we all become more and more conscious of what we want from ourselves, we are expecting more and more from our partners.

This is good! For too long, the world has provided us with its image for relationships, and now, people are beginning to develop their own model. But as we are growing and expecting more from ourselves and others, we need to also commit to seeing the relationship through the rough spots. I see many couples who break up right at the point of real growth because of the rigidity of their thinking. We need to expect more, but we also need to have compassion and commitment. We also need to become the kind of person that we want our partner to be. This means that if we want more love, we must be willing to give more love. If we want a committed, considerate, romantic, generous partner, we too must become committed, considerate, romantic and generous.

A special relationship is actually based on hate, not love. There is a thin veneer of what we *think* is love, but this "love" is actually hiding our hate, our fear, our prejudices and our judgments. It hides everything we hate about ourselves. And when that veneer of love gets threatened, when the underlying feelings begin to surface, then hate rears its ugly head. My father used to say,

"There is a thin line between love and hate. At any time, the love can suddenly erupt into anger and hatred."

He didn't know it, but what he was talking about was special relationships. The way to see if you are in a special relationship is to watch how you feel and react as your partner changes. When we are in a special relationship we fear change, because change may ruin the relationship and then we may be alone once again. And so control and manipulation are tools that are used in a special relationship. If these tools do not work and our partner continues to change, we will begin to hate them because it feels as if they are taking their love away. The divorce courts are full of people who started out in "love" and now hate each other. Indeed, they hate each other so much, that they are willing to go into financial bankruptcy and custody battles to "make the other person pay."

Exclusion is another hallmark of a special relationship. "You and me against the world, babe" is a common thought in a special relationship. The relationship is used to judge who is "in" and worthy of your love and who is "out" and not worthy of your love. Those of us who have experienced the pain, for example, of being in a clique in high school, know how quickly our *dearest* friends can turn on us, and how quickly we can go from being *in* to *out*. Exclusion provides a false sense of security or belonging. It's based on the concept that, "As long as you do not threaten my defenses or the status quo, you are loved."

Another indication of a special relationship is that the people involved are running what's called a "protection racket." A protection racket is what people do when they do not want to address what is really going on in their lives. The credo of a protection racket is, "I won't call you on your stuff if you won't call me on mine." It is based on the fear that if our partner saw all the ugly truths (actually they are untruths) about ourselves, they would not want to be with us. In fact, we fear, *nobody* would want to be with us. We feel broken and incomplete, and, since we think we are *both* broken, we agree not to talk about it so that nobody will get upset or threatened. It is based on the denial that anything is wrong. Or we don't address the issues because we unconsciously feel that this is all we deserve or we are afraid of being alone.

The last tool that the ego uses in special relationships is its favorite—projection. Here is how projection works. Let's say that you are feeling bad about yourself—maybe feeling guilty for past misdeeds, judging your fat thighs, feeling insecure about your balding head, or just plain hating yourself. The ego sidles up to you and says,

"Hey! You're feeling really bad! You know, I have a neat little trick that will take care of those feelings. All you have to do is throw them off on somebody else! Look at how bad everybody else is! Make them guilty, fat, balding or hateful. Then they'll have all the guilt and fear and you'll feel better."

And so we project our negative thoughts and feelings onto others and it *does* feel better—for awhile. We blame our partner for the very things we feel guilty about. We judge his or her looks, career or maturity and never try, as Susan Jeffers suggests in *Opening Our Hearts to Men*, "turning our magnifying glass into a mirror." In order to get rid of our unconscious guilt and fear, we project it onto the world—thereby seeing everybody else as guilty, fearful and hateful. As long as we blame our partner, as long as we project, nothing has to change. We can complain about our partner to our heart's content without ever having to look at our part in the situation.

The ego never tells you the cost of projection, which is that you will always get to feel like a victim because now it's everybody else's fault for what goes wrong in your life. It never tells you that you'll feel stuck—forever—until you stop projecting. It never tells you that your problems will never change, because the problems are not *out there*, they are inside you!

As you are reading all this about special relationships, are you feeling a little depressed? Maybe you're thinking, "God, I've done all those things! I'm so codependent! I'm so screwed up! Nothing will help!" I know I did the first time I saw the kind of relationships I had created. But dwelling on what we did wrong does not correct the error. We need another model, a new basis for relationships. And that model is called a holy relationship.

## The Holy (Wholly) Relationship

When many people hear the word "holy" they generally link it up to words like "sacred," "Godlike," "holier-than-thou," "asexual"— and "boring." You may even envision a monk, walking and meditating in a prayerful stance. So instead of seeing a holy relationship as sacred, or pertaining to God, change the word *holy* in your mind to *wholly*—a holy relationship is *wholly* loving, *wholly* fun, *wholly* sexual, *wholly* honest. It is a place where people experience more completeness and feel more whole.

A holy relationship is based on healing and love. Its goal is to heal, to see the wholeness of each person, despite the seeming flaws, and to acknowledge that each person is *already complete* and perfect in his or her own way. It is based on mutual empowerment, integrity and honesty. There are no secrets in a holy relationship, because secrets cause distance and kill love.

Both people know that they are not yet perfect and so they will continually be learning together. The purpose of a holy relationship is to get back to the love and truth—*no matter what*—even if we have to drop all of our projections and defenses. And so, when we are angry, sad, or jealous, we let our partner know, not in attack and blame, but with self-honesty, mutual trust and love. The purpose is not to make the other person wrong, but to find out something about ourselves, to clear the air and to return to the loving feelings we desire. Learning to do this takes time and practice, but then, that *is* all we have.

Having a holy relationship does not mean that people sing hymns and pray to God all day. It does not mean that my wife and I are in bliss and love every single moment. We still have arguments, worry about money, make dinner, have sex, feed the cat, commute to work and worry about our kids—just like anybody else. The difference, though, is that in a holy relationship we see all of these actions as ways that we can identify *our own triggers and projections*. We realize that these issues are opportunities to decide whether we want to be right or happy, whether we are willing to be defenseless and see another person's side, whether we can lower our barriers. These issues and how to address them will be covered in more detail later in this book.

Though it may take us some time when we are in the midst of a disagreement, we ultimately see that arguments are an *opportunity* to let go of our pride and the need to be right, and get to the Truth of the situation. Even when we sometimes feel resentful and tired, we then try to see our daily activities as an opportunity to express the love and caring we have for ourselves, each other, and the world.

A holy relationship *includes* the world. People in a holy relationship know that as they heal their issues with each other, they are also healing personal issues with themselves. As the relationship fosters more and more healing, their issues with the world are also handled. As you relate more lovingly with yourself and your partner, you will find that relating to your boss or customers is also easier. And, as you relate more and more lovingly to your boss or customers, you will find that relating with your partner is better.

As the special relationship is based on form, how it *looks*, the holy relationship is based on *content*, what's inside. The world tends to judge relationships on their form, whether you're going steady, dating, engaged, living together or married. Each stage has a different level of approval by the world. The world judges whether the relationship fits the form **it** approves of, and forms outside the accepted norm are judged as bad or against human nature. Gay, interracial, and relationships that cross religions are frowned upon and judged. The world sees gay/lesbian relationships as *unnatural*. The world sees a mixed marriage as *threatening* to **its** form and sends out the message that marriages not based on the same race or religion will never last. When both partners *unconsciously* agree that such relationships are hard or unnatural (our thoughts are always creating—see the next section), they naturally create more problems.

A holy relationship does not care about the form but only asks, "Is healing going on here? Is joy being expressed? Are these people having fun? Is there aliveness and compassion for each other?"

Whether the relationship is a long-term commitment or not, whether it is straight or gay, between a black person and a white person, between a Christian and a Muslim, the only thing that really matters is whether each person upholds the Divinity of the other while empowering them to be all that they can be. This leads to growth, healing and happiness.

The world may try to make us fit *its* form, but ultimately, it is *up to us* to address our own issues of self-doubt and low self-esteem. It is up to us to choose the life-style we desire. The real purpose of our relationships is to become **better people**, to learn to open up to others and to open up to ourselves. The first step in creating a loving relationship is to learn to love and accept yourself *just as you are*—regardless of your imperfections.

It's learning about loving and accepting the beautiful, wonderful, gay, straight, black, white, male, female, Christian, Muslim person. So many of us judge ourselves harshly, never realizing the beauty and splendor that is our True Self. A holy relationship gives us the opportunity to see that Self.

In the movie *Gandhi*, the Mahatma gives a man the chance to heal himself by creating a holy relationship. Gandhi is near death after a prolonged fast in opposition to the killings and hatred that have been going on between the Hindus and Muslims. After both warring sides finally come together in agreement and lay down their arms, a wild looking Hindu, tortured by guilt and hatred, breaks through the crowd and thrusts a piece of bread at Gandhi.

"Here! Eat! Get well! I will go to hell, but not with *your* life on my soul!"

"Why are you going to hell?" asks the weakened Mahatma.

"The Muslims! They killed my boy! And so," says the man, shaking under the pain and hurt, "I killed a Muslim boy—I smashed his head against a wall!"

Gandhi closes his eyes as the grief and sadness of the situation registers. The man is trembling in guilt, fear and rage. After a moment Gandhi replies.

"I know a way out of hell. Find a child. A Muslim child. About the same age as your son. A child whose parents have been killed. And raise him as your own. Only be sure you raise him—as a Muslim."

Gandhi knew the way out of hell was by seeing past the forms of religion and remembering the original purpose of religion—to love.

Another example of how form vs. content shows up is in relation to affairs. The world of form defines an affair as "having sex with another person." I have seen couples fight and argue over whether one of them had an affair because actual sexual contact was not made. She maintains her innocence because they never actually "did it." He feels hurt and betrayed because he feels that, at some level, they did. The holy relationship cuts through this bull! Since it looks at the content, the question no longer becomes,

"Was sexual contact made?" (*form*)

The new question becomes,

"Did this partner withdraw their emotions from their partner and become *emotionally involved* with another?" (*content*)

This is why we read more and more about Internet affairs. When a person thinks in terms of form, they may actually feel that there is nothing wrong, because the physical act was never completed. But in terms of emotional fidelity, the bond has been betrayed.

Initially, *all* relationships start as special relationships. We are attracted initially by a pretty face, a nice car, a vivacious personality or a calm persona. And at some unconscious level, we think this person is the answer to our dreams. We think the vivacious personality will fulfill us, never seeing the other sides of the personality.

When I was unconscious, I saw myself as a basically loving, huggable type of guy. I was not afraid to show my feelings or affection. But at that time, it was an *act*. It was a way that I found that women related to me and I hardly ever had a problem getting a woman to believe it—for a while. But over time, the suppressed aspects of myself would become activated, and the scared man who controlled and manipulated slowly emerged. Though I still *looked* and *acted* like a loving man, I was always making sure my partner felt as if she owed me something. Not surprisingly, my partner would begin to resent me. She would find herself wanting to "rip my head off" for no apparent reason.

What was being activated in my partner were the suppressed feelings that I was trying to control and prevent her from seeing in me, but she would see them anyway. Ultimately, we got into fights and would end the relationship, each feeling wronged by the other.

When I began to practice turning over my relationships to God in order to create holy relationships, it seemed that, for a while, nothing I did was right. This was because my past "methods" no longer worked. You see, when you suddenly change the goal of your relationships from codependency, secretiveness, fear and trying to *get* from another person, to openness, honesty, love and healing, your world feels upside down. There are not many role models from which to learn. We may be tempted to go back to our old, special relationship, however, this is now the time to trust.

If we persist, if we persevere in remembering where we want to go and remember to take steps toward the love we want to feel, we will see that we are not alone. There are others who have been where we are, others who have felt what we feel. We can find a mentor to help us along the way. They can guide us through.

Remember that your partner can become a mighty companion, as you both claim the life and love you deserve. Once we open to love, we are never alone, for we now have God on our side.

# Self Discovery Quiz

- *Do you feel fear whenever your partner proposes a change in his/her life? Are you afraid of them succeeding or failing? Is your self-worth tied into their self-worth?*

- *Is your relationship growing or has it leveled out to a point of complacency?*

- *Does your relationship feed your soul?*

- *Do you feed your partner's soul?*

- *Do you feel excited and passionate about your relationship?*

- *Are the both of you blessed because of your relationship?*

- *Is there something that your partner does that abuses your spirit? Do you want to do anything about it? What will you do? When will you confront the situation?*

- *What is the worst thing that could happen if you claimed the type of relationship you've always desired? What is the best thing that could happen?*

- *Are you afraid of telling your partner about something that irritates you about him/her, because they may tell you all of the things that you do to irritate him/her? How long do you want to stay in this pattern?*

- *How can you take a step today toward creating a relationship that feeds your soul?*

*You got to be very careful
if you don't know where you're going,
because you might not get there.*

**Yogi Berra**


*I never hold a grudge,
especially when I'm wrong.*

**Oscar Levant**


*Hating people is like
burning down your own house
to get rid of a rat.*

**Harry Emerson Fosdick**


*What a wonderful life I've had!
I only wish I'd realized it sooner.*

**Colette**

# If You Don't Know Where You're Going, How Will You Know When You've Arrived?

Typically, most of us start endeavors or get into relatioships without knowing why we are doing them. We "fall" in love. The job just seems to "drop" into our lap. Things just seem to "happen" to us. We don't really know why we are doing what we are doing, and then we complain about the outcome, that the relationship didn't work out or that our jobs are not fulfilling.

Sometimes when I am talking to a person about their hopes and dreams for a new relationship, I hear statement such as:

"I hope I do better this time. . . . I *think* this is my perfect partner, I *hope* it works out. . . . All my past relationships failed but I hope I'm better this time. . . . I hope I don't make the same mistakes like last time."

When I ask these people exactly what solid steps they are going to take to create a better relationship, they are stumped. They haven't given much thought to *exactly* what they want and even less on what they are willing to do to attain their goal.

Let me ask you something. If the CEO of IBM gave these types of statements to his/her Board of Directors, how long would he/she stay as a CEO?

"Here's our business plan for 1999. I *hope* it goes well. We made a lot of mistakes last year, but I'm sure it will be better this year. At least I *think* it will. We are going to have to borrow money for expenses, but we'll be able to pay it back. . . somehow. That is my plan."

When we get into a relationship (or any other endeavor), most of us neglect to ask ourselves the questions,

*"What do I want to come of this? What is it for?"*

**Text** pg. 340 / 366 [Author's bolding]

Without a clear-cut, predefined goal set at the beginning, situations just **seem to happen.** Things go wrong and we don't know how to respond and so instead of responding, we react. We have no criterion for what we should do or what needs to be corrected because we don't know why we're doing it in the first place!

It's like going into an empty field and digging this deep, square hole. After awhile, the walls start crumbling in or rain washes the sides down. We keep digging fruitlessly until we finally give up in despair. And then we go into another field and start all over again. This is how many of my relationships used to evolve: digging a hole in the ground with no real idea why I was doing it, struggling, failing, and then starting over again.

But what if your purpose of digging in that field is to build a house? Now you have a goal. And so, any interference between you and that completed house can now be handled, because you will be concentrating on your goal of a completed house, not just digging some vague, square hole. As the *Course* states:

> *The value of deciding in advance what you want to happen is simply that you will perceive the **situation as a means to make it happen**. You will therefore make **every effort** to **overlook** what interferes with the accomplishment of your objective, and **concentrate** on everything that helps you meet it.*

Text pg. 340 / 366 [Author's bolding]

So when the walls start to crumble, instead of saying, "This does not work. I think I'll quit and start over," you'll ask yourself,

"*Why* am I doing this? Is my goal to dig a deep, square hole, with walls that crumble? No! My goal is to build a house. So, what do I need to do to complete the task?"

And you'll hire men to pour a foundation and shore up the walls. Instead of every problem threatening the task, every problem now merely needs to be addressed and corrected, one by one. In fact, every problem can lead you to a better and stronger outcome. When the plumbing is not right or the roof leaks, you'll come back to your goal.

"Is my goal to have a house that leaks or plumbing that does not work? No! What do I need to do to fix it?"

And then you'll hire roofers and plumbers (or learn to do it yourself) and correct the problem. Your focus is now aimed toward **success**, as opposed to *just doing*.

When love and healing are the goals in your relationship, you'll begin to see problems in a new way. Instead of the problem always threatening the relationship, you'll now see the problem as something that is interfering with the love and healing. You'll ask yourself,

"Is the purpose of our relationship to fight about money or argue about my mother? Is that why we got together? No! Our purpose is to love and appreciate each other. Our purpose is to get back to the love. So what do we need to do to get back to the love?"

And you will do anything to correct it. You may call a friend, minister or a counselor. You may take workshops or read books. You may even change your mind about yourself or the other person. You may even admit when you're wrong. When love becomes the focus, you will begin to see that no problem is too big to be solved. You will discover that it is actually better to be wrong and happy than right and miserable.

Committing to healing ourselves will also draw to us loving, and sometimes funny, ways for us to heal. Because even when I forget my goal, even when I am adamant in my views, since I have set up love and healing as my goal, the Holy Spirit remembers and gently reminds me.

One morning, early in our marriage, Stav and I had a really furious fight—I don't even remember what the argument was about—but I was *hating* her. I had finally decided that this relationship was **not** going to work and I was shutting her out. As far as I was concerned, she was dead, gone—a nobody. I was lying in bed, my back to her and my arms crossed. I had my eyes (and mind) closed and my "shields on full." You know, the traditional surrender position. She was behind me, rubbing my shoulder and trying to help me see differently.

"Come on, Jerry. It's not that bad. Turn around and look at me. We need to talk about this."

But as far as I was concerned, she was dead. She proceeded to love me but I resisted. Suddenly the phone rang and I answered it. It was one of my clients. He was having a fight—with his wife.

And so, there I was, still angry with my wife, lying in bed, listening to this man pour out this story on how his wife didn't understand him, how he was wronged, etc. After a few moments I interjected,

"So, Bill, what resistance are you having to seeing your wife's side? Is it possible that she really loves you and you're just not willing to see it? What are you really afraid of?"

I could see out of the corner of my eye that Stav was smiling. I tried to resist it but I started smiling too. I continued with my support.

"Can you open up to the hurt little child inside of you," I asked, "and tell your wife what you want? Can you tell her how you too are hurt?"

As I talked to him, I began to see how shut down and crazy I was. I also began to feel how hurt and lonely I felt when I held onto my righteousness. I supported him for a few more minutes and then hung up the phone.

"Who was it?" asked Stav.

"The Holy Spirit," I replied.

We both burst into laughter.

One very simple goal-setting technique that Stav and I use every New Year's Eve is to spend some time together developing our goals for the coming year. We give ourselves some quiet time, light some candles, say a prayer, give thanks for the past year and decide what we want to attain in the coming year. We list our spiritual, financial and material goals, bless them and see these goals reached. Throughout the following year we will take out these goals and review them, to keep adding power and energy toward attaining these goals.

Sometimes, though, we have forgotten to review the list, even forgetting what we had originally listed. But what we have found is that setting the goals and then releasing them releases any energy in *having* to accomplish these goals. The very act of making a list plants the seeds and we know that they will germinate.

The following New Years Eve we get out the goals for that year and review how we did. What is surprising is how many goals we actually forgot we had, and how many goals were reached. One year Stav wanted to put "Buy a new car" on our list.

"But we don't have enough money," I argued. "I don't see how we could possibly get one."

"It's not going to hurt to put a new car on our list. Let's just see what happens."

So, grudgingly, I agreed, certain that this goal could not be attained. The seed was planted even though over the ensuing months both of us completely forgot that goal. During the year we not only surpassed our financial goals, but we also bought a brand new car, on December 10th. When we opened up our yearly goals notebook and read what we had visualized for that year, we were surprised to find that we had asked for a new car.

I have since learned that there is no request that is too hard or impossible, when two people put their minds to it. This leads to the main point of this chapter:

# Creating a Purpose and Goals

A very powerful tool that we use frequently in all important endeavors is developing a *Purpose and Goals Statement* for the intended task. This tool briefly outlines why you are doing what you are doing, and the expected outcomes.

The Purpose section of a Purpose and Goals Statement is usually short, one or two sentences. It states the purpose of this endeavor and the *general direction* that you want to take. The purpose may or may not actually ever be reached. One example of such a purpose is "to travel east." You can never finish traveling east, but it does indicate the direction you are going.

A relationship purpose could be, "to support and empower each other to be all that we can be." Once again, this purpose states the general direction that we want the relationship to go. It may be quite a while before this purpose is attained, but that doesn't matter. It is the direction that guides us.

The Goals section of a Purpose and Goals Statement lists *specific* goals that are desired. These goals are a number of tasks or results that can actually be measured and attained. Setting goals helps us determine how well we approached our purpose. Goals can be: to listen to each other, to take a breath whenever we are upset and defensive, to not storm out of the house in anger when we have an argument, or to be willing to try on a new idea. In this way, you can actually verify whether you are succeeding in the areas that are important to you. If you are not, then you can fine-tune your strategy. An example of a Purpose and Goals for a relationship may look like:

# Purpose and Goals for Our Relationship

## *Purpose*

> *To have a loving, dynamic relationship that helps to*
> *see the Christ in each other, to increase the fun, love*
> *and peace in our lives. To heal any unresolved issues*
> *that we have.*

## *Goals*

- *To enjoy each other's company*
- *To have passionate, exciting sex*
- *To publicly acknowledge our love for each other*
- *To ask for help when we get into a fight and can't*
  *resolve it ourselves*
- *To spend at least two nights a week in quality*
  *time connecting*
- *To tell each other what we want instead of*
  *keeping our partner guessing*
- *To take a vacation to Hawaii*
- *To practice defenselessness when my partner is*
  *communicating an upset*

A fundamental principle that my wife and I live by and teach is that our thoughts create the world we live in (see Law #1 in the next section). When we formulate Purpose and Goals, what we are doing is focusing the power of our *combined* thoughts toward a common end. It starts the wheels of creativity turning. It also provides us with a road map. As you can see by the previous example, our Purpose is a direction that we will be following for a long time. Healing our unresolved issues is an ongoing process.

However, the Goals can be measured. Even if we don't succeed in some of our Goals, we can examine what happened, what went wrong and we can try again. If we are sincere in our intentions to have a dynamic, healthy, loving relationship, we must honor the Goals and agreements. If we don't, we are lying to ourselves about our real agenda. We must be willing to walk the walk and use our Purpose and Goals as our compass.

The other advantage to the Purpose and Goals is that it gives both partners a sense of safety. Since most of us get into relationships with lots of wounds, particularly abandonment, having agreements and a common Purpose and Goals helps ease some of the anxiety. Fears about the other will ease more and more as we practice consistency and integrity in our behavior and interactions. This also allows both people to build a sense of trust for the other as they see their partner keeping their word. For another powerful tool, see the chapter later in this book entitled "Commit or Get Off the Pot."

Purpose and Goals may be used to help you to find the relationship you want or improve the one you currently have. I have found that the reason I wouldn't list my purpose, desires and goals was because I was afraid I would have to change something once I realized I wasn't getting what I wanted in my relationships. Also, in the beginning, I had no idea of what I wanted. All I knew was what I didn't want. Many of us believe "that things should just *happen*." A Purpose and Goals Statement helps you to get detailed and to focus on what you **do want**.

Make love the purpose and goal in all of your endeavors. It doesn't matter what you do for a living, whether you're a CEO of IBM or a waitress at Denny's. Ask yourself,

"Why am I *truly* here? Is the purpose of my life to make just enough money to pay the bills and the rent, so that I have a place to sleep, so that I can rest up and be ready to work once again at a job I don't like? Am I only here to *make a buck*? Or am I here to experience more joy in my life, express my creativity, learn to love myself and others **and** live prosperously?"

Regarding your relationships, ask yourself,

"Why am I truly in this relationship? Is the purpose of my relationships to stave off the loneliness I feel, to control my partner, to make me feel a little better for awhile and then to break up? Am I destined to spend my life seeking but never finding a good relationship? Or can I have fun, love and dreams while I push back my ego, while I mature into the type of person that I would love to be in a relationship with? Can committing to finding the love that has always been present give me the love and peace I have always desired?"

Give yourself a goal that you are *guaranteed* of achieving someday—opening up to love. And don't do it alone. Open up to God and let Him help. When you do, no problem or situation will ever again be as big. As Maya Angelou stated in her book, *Wouldn't Take Nothing for My Journey Now,*

"For what could stand against me with God, since one person, *any person with God*, constitutes the majority."

# *Affirmations*

- *I am now willing to see there is a larger reason for the relationships I create.*

- *I now become more intentional in how I handle my relationships.*

- *I am willing to see the whole truth about myself, even if it is wonderful.*

- *I am willing to see the whole truth about my partner, even if it is wonderful.*

- *I now take responsibility for the results I create in my relationships.*

- *I now stop trying to control my life and my relationships. I now give God permission to work in my life and in my relationships.*

- *My heart is big enough to allow my relationship, my family, my friends and my world to fit into it.*

- *I no longer think I need to keep my relationships separate from the rest of my life.*

- *My goal is to always return to the love.*

- *I no longer expect my partner to have to choose between me and his/her family and friends.*

*Nothing is more destined to create
deep-seated anxieties in people than the false
assumption that life should be free of anxiety.*
**Archbishop Fulton J. Sheen**


*It is easier to love humanity as a whole
than to love one's neighbor.*
**Eric Hoffer**


*If you have come to help me,
you are wasting your time.
But if you have come because
your liberation is bound up with mine,
then let us work together.*
**Words of an aboriginal Australian woman**


*Love can sweep you off your feet
and carry you along in a way
you've never known before.
But the ride always ends,
and you end up feeling
lonely and bitter.
Wait.
It's not love I'm describing.
I'm thinking of a monorail.*
**Jack Hendey**

# How Relationships Evolve

Something my wife and I have learned in our trainings and in our personal and professional relationships is that all relationships progress through five basic stages. Knowing that there is a natural progression in our relationships can help alleviate a lot of fears and disappointments. These stages are:

- Individuality
- Competition
- Compromise
- Cooperation
- Synergy

Most relationships never get past competition or compromise. For many people it seems like too much effort to work past those stages because their egos will not allow it or they just don't know a better way. If the partners persist in staying together, but do no work on their feelings of competition or sacrifice (compromise), it will feel like an armed camp—each defensive side afraid of losing ground or afraid that the other person is dominating.

In these early stages, people are operating from a primal directive of survival and a fear of the other, and our motives are to protect and defend. We are not yet at a point where we feel that we can relax our defenses and open our minds to other possibilities. Attaining the stages of cooperation and synergy requires trust, defenselessness and surrender, which will be covered in later chapters in this book.

# Individuality

In this stage each person still tries to hold onto their separateness in an attempt to preserve who they *think* they are. They resent any infraction into their *territory*. They have secret fears, doubts and judgments and are resistant to sharing them. They think that *they know best*.

Now, this does not mean that in a good relationship both people are just part of an egoless blob. In a good relationship, both partners still have their individuality, but they realize there are times that their individuality can actually get in the way and harm the relationship by fostering separation. As Glenda Greene (a spiritual teacher) states,

"There is a fine line where the two become one and the one becomes two. That is a holy place. When both partners can honor it, the relationship is very strong."

# Competition (Power and Control)

Whereas, at first the relationship looks like two individuals who just *happen* to love each other, now these individuals are trying to share a life. The basic low self-esteem and doubts that lurk within each person now really start to surface. As each partner *perceives* the possible loss of love, they begin to compete for it. They compete for control, for time, for love, for the remote control, for the stations on the radio—for anything that comes to mind. Competition is an *unacknowledged fear of the loss of love* that is then acted out. Competition is where we recreate and reenact our relationships with our parents and siblings and then project our defenses onto our partner.

Competition is based on the thought that in order for me to win, somebody has to lose. When you come from this belief, then every time you win (get a promotion, get your perfect relationship, win the lottery), it will bring up feelings of guilt (in most cases, unconscious guilt). And since we feel that somebody had to lose in order for us to win, we feel unconsciously responsible for the other person. Continuous competition ultimately leads to low self-esteem, feelings of paranoia and even self-sabotage. In the business world, I have seen people compete tooth and nail for a better career and then sabotage their success because of unconscious guilt resulting from constantly competing and never facing the resulting feelings of guilt. In this way they can *pay off their guilt* by losing their money.

In the movie *Streets of Gold*, the turning point occurs when a fighter lets go of his competition with a teammate. The movie is about two U.S. boxers, a black man and a white man who are trained by an exiled Jewish, Russian boxer. Both men are good, but it soon becomes obvious that the black boxer is the better of the two. During their training, the two men initially compete with each other—each one trying to outdo the other. Over time, though, they begin to respect each other's qualities and finally become friends. They prove themselves in amateur competition and both get the opportunity to represent the United States against a visiting Russian boxing team.

Then, in a twist of fate, the black man gets injured in a street fight and the white boxer must now fight alone. Because it was an ex-friend of the white boxer who injured his teammate, he now feels guilty for making it to the ring alone. Even though the white boxer is good, his own low self-esteem, compounded with his guilt saps his confidence in himself.

During the boxing match, his punches just aren't effective and the Russian boxer is clearly winning. And then, just before the last round, the black boxer, with his hand bandaged from his wound, leaves his spectator's seat, comes down toward the ring, makes eye contact with his friend, and tells him,

"There's enough room at the top for both of us. Take him *down*!"

And, of course, once the boxer sees that his friend wants him to win, he drops his guilt and gives it his all, winning the match.

When my wife and I do a workshop, we have learned the value of being aware of *all* of our competitive thoughts with each other, so that we do not act them out in front of our audience. To become more aware, we share our individual fears with each other before the workshop. Fears such as

"Everybody will love you more than me."

"You'll look better than me."

"All my clients will think that you are better than me."

Most of the time we find we have the same fears. This sharing is a way we can clear out our fears and acknowledge any competition we may be feeling. Later, as my partner is doing her part in the workshop and she's doing great and all eyes are on her, I sometimes feel the need to interject my own thoughts, to "illuminate" a topic. I have realized, though, that at these moments, I am in fear and feel that I may be *losing* everybody's love. I want to shine and remind everybody that "I am here too!"

I have realized now that this is just competition, and so I take a silent breath and remind myself that I am safe and loved just for who I am, not for what I do or say. Then I offer my idea up to God, knowing that if it *needs* to be said, it will be said. Many times I have seen that as I let go of the thought, my partner will then present that same idea as part of her speech. Or, she'll turn to me and ask if there's anything I would like to add. And at that point I am being reminded that, "there's enough room at the top for both of us."

## *Compromise*

This word comes from Latin, which means "to promise together." It is a mutual promise between two people to uphold an agreement. Although compromise is a necessary stage in bettering your relationship, it ultimately does not work. It is not satisfying. Can you remember a time when you compromised on a subject? Didn't you feel that *somehow* you got the short end of the stick?

Compromise is always based on the concept that **you** have to sacrifice something and **I** have to sacrifice something for the greater good. Compromise expects both parties to sacrifice and is actually a "lose-lose" scenario. In the end, both sides usually feel cheated. A statement that emphasizes compromise is the adage, "A half loaf is better than none." This may be true if you are starving but it does not work in relationships. Too many times I see couples compromise what they desire only to receive half of what they wanted. Ultimately, each person then feels cheated and resentful.

In the movie *The Mirror Has Two Faces*, we see Barbara Streisand compromise for a relationship that she doesn't believe in because she believes that she is not pretty enough and has to settle for what *he wants* in the relationship. But over time the pain of not having what she wants (a man who loves her romantically and sexually) grows so intense that finally she leaves him. She's tired of " a half loaf" and wants all or nothing. When her husband realizes what it is she wants, when he realizes that he *does* love her but is afraid of opening once again to a woman, he finally surrenders to his own love and acknowledges his love for her.

The real reason compromise does not work is because there is still a feeling of separateness between the partners. There is still an "us" against "them" mentality: each side trying to get the most out of the situation. There is still no *common* goal. There is only a secret desire to get our way, whether it supports the relationship or not.

Although compromise is based on separateness and a lose-lose scenario, it is still a *positive step* toward a better relationship, because at this point, each partner is willing to give toward the other. However, our ultimate goal is to learn and practice giving without either party losing.

## Cooperation

This is a step in which the parties begin to see themselves as part of a team or partners; when one wins, the other benefits, and when one loses, so does the other. Now, instead of trying to scrounge a little personal sense of winning, both partners look for how both people can win. This is the beginning of the *win-win* scenario.

In order for a win-win to evolve, ***both parties* must be willing for *each person* to get what they want.** That means that both sides feel that they have won without anybody sacrificing. In Gay and Kathlyn Hendricks' book, *Conscious Loving*, they give an example of how a couple that they were working with resolved an argument. The man's mother watched as her son and daughter-in-law shared feelings, mirrored back to each other how they were feeling and what they wanted. It was a lengthy process of telling the truth and unraveling what the issues were *really* about, but finally they got back to the love and agreement. At this point the mother asked them,

"OK, I see how this works, but how do you know who won?"

The mother was obviously still in competition mode, thinking that every disagreement must be won or lost.

In cooperation, the partners establish goals and they set rules and guidelines for the attainment of those goals. They support each individual toward the attainment of any *personal* goal, supporting each other's dreams and desires, because it also supports the relationship. There is less *me* and more *us*. Individuals are still needed to express desires and wants, but the individual is no longer a roadblock.

More about the win-win example will be explained later in the book.

## *Synergy*

This is an experience where the total contribution of both individuals is greater than if you had added each partner's contribution individually. For example, one plus one equals two, but when synergy is involved, there is a greater pooling of our inner resources and now one plus one equals three—something greater than two! That is because at this stage, the partners now know that there is a larger presence in their lives. They realize that the relationship is not dependent on their tiny bits of knowledge but upon a greater

*Knowing*, that there is **always** an answer to any conflict and all they need do is share their truths, open their hearts and let their Divine selves lend a hand. This is where the "win-win" concept really bears fruit.

To achieve synergy, though, a relationship must go through each of the preceding stages, no matter how many years you have been practicing having a conscious relationship.

A few years ago, Stav and I were planning a three week vacation and couldn't agree on where to go. I wanted to go to Seattle, to introduce her to my friends, the mountains and the islands. **She** wanted to be on a sunny beach (*Individuality*). We began to argue the merits of each position trying to convince the other that we had the better plan (*Competition*). So we went to a travel agent to see what was available and to book a flight. During the discussion with the agent, it seemed as if Seattle would be the cheapest and easiest, and so, even though Stav didn't totally agree, we booked a flight to Seattle (*Compromise*).

Luckily, we had an alert travel agent who perceived that we were really not at ease with our decision, and so she told us that she would reserve our seats, but would not write the ticket until the next morning to give us time to think about it. We agreed and left for a dinner engagement with a friend who had just flown in from San Diego.

On the way to dinner, we decided that neither of us felt good about the outcome. I felt guilty for getting my way, and Stav felt disappointed and somewhat resentful because she still wanted to go to the beach. And so we decided to release the trip as it was and see if there was a higher plan. We offered our vacation to God and asked Him to help us.

As we drove, Stav shared her feelings.

"Jerry, this has been such a hard year for us. I just want to relax. I need to be in the sun and be pampered. We've worked so hard and we need this rest. It doesn't have to be the whole trip, but

I do want us to spend *some* time on the beach. What is it you really want?"

"What I really want is mountains. It's been years since I've seen snow-covered mountains, glaciers and valleys, and I miss them. That is what's important to me. The friends in Seattle we can see anytime, but right now my soul yearns to be in the mountains. And it doesn't have be the whole trip either, but I do want *some* time in the mountains."

Just then I had a thought.

"You know," I said, "Jay and Sandra (our friends) live in Colorado. What would happen if we drove up there and stayed with them? We can visit the mountains for a week and a half and then drive back to Texas and spent the rest of the time on Padre Island, on the Gulf Coast."

Stav thought about it and agreed. It felt like we had found the way to have our mountains *and* our beach (*Cooperation*). But there was more to come.

Later, while having dinner with our friend, Robin, we told him about our vacation decision and he piped up.

"You know, guys, I'm going to be out of town during that period. If you want, you can fly into San Diego from Colorado instead of driving back to Texas and stay at my apartment and use my car. I live only a few blocks from the beach."

And so we altered our plans. We drove to Colorado, had a nice visit with our friends, and I got to see my snow-covered mountains and elk. For a few days we rented a little cottage by a rushing stream and watched droves of hummingbirds as they fed at the feeders. I love hummingbirds and I didn't realize that they were so prolific that time of year. It was an unexpected bonus for me. We both felt refreshed and rejuvenated and enjoyed the mountains immensely. Then we flew from Colorado to San Diego and spent another ten days in the sun. We also went to Disneyland, which was a dream Stav had had for years. It was an unexpected bonus for Stav.

The outcome of the trip was due to *Synergy*. Not only did we get what we both wanted, but we got more! And with greater ease!

Does this mean that once you reach synergy, you're finished? Your relationship is perfect and you can now relax? No! Of course not! Couples may be married for many years and practice these rules and still have to go through individuality, competition, compromise, cooperation and synergy whenever they have a disagreement. The only difference now is that it doesn't take as long to come up with a final solution that works. As couples give themselves more and more practice and hold steadfast to the principle that *no one has to lose* in order for them to get what they want, creative solutions are found. The steps come easier and easier. What could take days to resolve now takes hours or even minutes, and each time the couple learns a little bit more about themselves. Relationships present us with "unlimited opportunities to grow" because we are given new opportunities to embrace our larger, loving selves. This is what it means to heal.

Don't be afraid to let your relationships grow and change. As you open to the love that is all around you, as you open to the wisdom that is within, you and your partner will find each step is loving, safe, and gentle. It's the resistance to letting go of control and changing our minds that causes the problems, the stress and the fear. It is our insistence on being right rather than happy that keeps us locked into no-win situations and power struggles.

So take a chance.

Take a breath.

And take your steps.

# Self Discovery Quiz

- *Which stage of relationship do you think you are currently in? Where would you like it to be? When would you like to take the next step?*

- *What would be a step you could take that would take your relationship to the next level?*

- *What thoughts, feelings or old hurts are between you and your next step? Who would you need to forgive in order to let your partner's love in even more?*

- *Have you ever done anything in your past that sabotaged a relationship? What was it? Can you forgive yourself now and make plans on how not to repeat the error again?*

- *Are you more interested in getting your way or being happy?*

- *Do you keep repeating patterns because you are afraid of losing control?*

- *If your partner had total control of your life, what are you afraid he/she would do?*

- *If you had total control of your partner's life, what are you afraid you would do?*

- *Have you known anybody who has a relationship that works? When was the last time you took them out for coffee, just to be with them and see how they relate?*

# The Laws of Relationships

The universe becomes a friendlier place to live in once we learn the spiritual laws that operate in it. Until then, the universe seems mysterious, obstinate, unloving and random. The world that we see through our eyes is what we *believe* is out there. However, the world we see is only the result of whatever spiritual laws we choose to obey or ignore. When we know the laws and follow them, the world makes more sense. For example, in the physical realm, we may not like the law of gravity, but when we understand and respect it, we now know how to use it.

*Some of the world's greatest feats were accomplished by people not smart enough to know they were impossible.*

**Doug Larson**

*All you need is to tell a man that he is no good ten times a day, and very soon he begins to believe it himself.*

**Lin Yutang**

*The great thing in this world is not so much where we are, but in what direction we are moving.*

**Oliver Wendell Holmes, Sr.**

*There once was a farmer who was missing his ax. He suspected the neighbor boy had taken it. And when the farmer next saw the boy, the boy looked like a thief, walked like a thief and talked like a thief. Later that week the farmer found his ax among some old tools that he had misplaced, and the next time the farmer saw his neighbor's son, the boy walked, looked and spoke like any other child.*

**Traditional German tale**

# Law #1:
# *"My Thoughts Create"*

**A** *Course in Miracles* states,

> *The mind is very powerful, and never loses its creative force. It never sleeps. Every instant it is creating....There are no idle thoughts.All thinking produces form at some level.*
>
> **Text pg. 26 / 30**

If we want to understand the world we live in and why things *happen* to us, we need to realize that our minds are continually creating and that whatever is in our minds will come to us. This pertains to our conscious thoughts *and* our unconscious thoughts.

When God created us, He gave us the same creative ability that He has. That means that every thought we have vibrationally and magnetically creates something. This creation can occur at the physical level, the emotional level, the spiritual level, the psychic level, or at any other levels (or dimensions) that we have yet to discover.

If you are new to this concept, it may help to imagine your thoughts as radio waves traveling out, looking for a receiving station. The people or situations that are at the same frequency as our thoughts will be attracted (tuned in) to our frequency and will be attracted toward us. And so, whatever we believe, spend time thinking about, perceive and expect—we get!

We have spent many years miscreating with our minds. We fret about the future, worry about the bills, worry if our lover is having an affair, mull over past hurts, complain about our upbringing, and, with all this effort being spent on negative, disempowering thoughts, we then wonder why our lives don't work. When we let our minds wander too much, without any discipline, we end up with chaos.

Since the problem is in our minds, the only place that any lasting change can be accomplished is in our minds. A miracle, according to *A Course in Miracles,* is **a change in perception.** The choices I make with my powerful, creative mind determines the world I think I live in. It is then my perception of the world that chooses what I create next. As I change my perception of the people in my life, I will relate to them differently, and they, in turn, will relate to me differently. If I relate with openness and an innocent perception, the situation will get better. If I relate with fear and suspicion, the situation will worsen.

Have you ever noticed how fear and paranoia feed on themselves? One day, after working out at the gym, I unlocked my locker to find it totally empty! Initially I was stunned, but then I began to get angry. Some *scumbag* had stolen everything! My clothes, shoes, wallet, gym bag—even my dirty socks! I was furious!

Not only did the perpetrator steal my belongings, but they also had the *audacity* to relock my locker with my own combination lock. I sat there fuming, trying to figure out what the hell to do, who to yell at, or what to punch. Then an inner voice spoke.

"You're wrong. That's not what happened at all."

I took a breath, gathered my senses and opened the locker *next* to the one I had locked. There were my clothes, shoes, wallet, gym bag—even my dirty socks. It took me a minute to realize that **I** had put the lock on the **wrong** locker. I had locked an empty locker!

I had made a mistake, and if I had not listened to my little voice, my fear and paranoia would have convinced me that there was a thief loose on the premises. It's possible that I would rant and rave at the management, maybe even accuse a fellow member. And, from that basis, I would begin to create more and more negative experiences based on that faulty belief.

Now you might be saying, "Well, if thoughts create, all I have to do is change my thoughts and then everything will get better. But

I've tried changing my thoughts. I did affirmations and took work-shops, and they seemed to help for a little while, but then the effects wore off. Why is that?"

There are two reasons for this happening. The first reason is that at first things seem to get better because the ego *does not know* what is initially happening. It's curious and lets down its guards, just a little. As the Course says,

> *The ego is therefore capable of suspiciousness at best, viciousness at worst.*
>
> **Text pg. 164 / 176**

And so maybe you try therapy, affirmations or a workshop. The ego lets you go on because it does not know what to expect. In my work as a Breath Integration Practitioner, it is not uncommon for a client to come in the first time and have a fantastic breath session. They may cry, rage and emote like they never did before. They may feel this surge of love flooding their body and when they leave, they swear that the session was the best thing that ever happened to them. They will be back.

And then, over the next few days, the ego kicks in and moves from suspiciousness to viciousness. It begins to assail the client with all kinds of doubts, fears and judgments. The client wonders whether these changes are really lasting, if he/she can really trust me, if I will hurt him/her. And the next session becomes more of a struggle, because now the client is coming from fear—fear of change, fear of the un-known, fear of going deeper within and confronting their own demons. And so out of fear and doubt, they stop working on themselves, they stop doing affirmations, they stop walking into the fear.

The second reason that positive changes are so often tempo-rary is that we must not only change our conscious thoughts, but also our unconscious thoughts. It has been estimated that the aver-age person has around 50,000 thoughts every day—and most of them are repetitive, negative self-talk. As you begin to work on your-self, only the conscious thoughts are addressed initially. And for awhile things seem to get better. But over time, the deep, unconscious thoughts begin to be addressed, and how you *really feel* about your issues begins to surface. You see, every unconscious thought we have is attached to an emotion, generally an uncomfortable emotion, an emotion we judge. The fact that we do not like this emotion is the original reason that we suppressed it in the first place. It is why we went *unconscious* to start with—to ignore or deny that this feeling even exists.

This is the time that we need to stick to our guns. Continue the affirmations, the therapy, the meditation, the yoga postures no matter what. No matter how bad you feel, no matter how bad your life looks, continue working on yourself until the old thoughts are released.

This is one way of addressing your unconscious thoughts. Another method of becoming aware of your unconscious thoughts is to look at your world, because the world *you see* is an accurate reflection of every thought you have. Is it a kind world? Is it a loving world? Or do you see a world peopled by persons only interested in themselves, who step on others and who don't care? What you focus on and *see* in your world tells you what you *believe* in. And what you believe in, you create.

I once saw a video of Lazaris, a very powerful and loving, channeled entity, who instructed us on how to recognize the thoughts we had that were creating the world we lived in. What he said was that whenever we felt stuck and couldn't see how the world reflected our thoughts, we were to ask ourselves,

"What kind of thoughts would I **have** to have in order to create the kind of life I now lead? If I work at a boring, depressing job, what kind of thoughts would I **have to have** to create that job? Do I believe that jobs are meant to be boring? Is work supposed to be hard or easy? Who told me these beliefs in the first place?"

As you look at your current relationship, ask yourself,

"Is this the kind of relationship I desire?"

If not, ask yourself what thoughts would a person **have to have** in order to create this type of relationship. When I started looking at the kinds of thoughts I had to have in order to create the relationships I had, I was a bit shocked. But it also made sense. I had thoughts like:

"Women cannot be trusted."

"Women will hurt me."

"You gotta sacrifice to be in a relationship."

"You can never understand women."

"Women are only interested in your looks, money or status."

As I became aware that it was my own thoughts that attracted me to the type of women I created in my life, I began to give myself new thoughts—thoughts that were aimed toward the kind of relationships I wanted. I gave myself affirmations (see the last chapter) to reaffirm the new thoughts I wanted, such as:

"I now know that women can be trusted because I can be trusted."

"Women only want to love me."

"I no longer sacrifice my desires, and I no longer expect my partner to sacrifice her desires.

"As I begin to understand myself, I find women understandable."

"Women are more loving than I ever thought."

And then, besides just doing affirmations to change my thinking, I took the next step to cement the new thoughts in my mind. I realized that all the affirmations in the world were not capable of bringing women into my apartment to meet me. And so I began to act *as if* those affirmations were true!

I started asking women out, with the idea that they only wanted to love me. I began to trust women more, knowing that it was my own self I was really trusting. I began to ask for what I wanted, trusting that my date would also ask for what she wanted. I began to expect the best from women. And as I discovered the best in women, I also found the best in me.

# The Role of Feelings in Our Creations

The second element that is used in creating your reality is your emotions. The mind, or the thinking part, sets the path that we want to follow. However, our true feelings are the *power* that **moves** us along that path. Feelings drive the thoughts.

Have you ever had an incident, where you tried to lose weight or get a new job, and, after many futile, halfhearted attempts, you finally got *really* mad? And now, you've had it! You were not a wimp anymore! You were finally determined and you drew that line in the sand and told your ego to get in line! Did you notice how suddenly the world seemed to listen? You were not tempted by food, because now your thoughts *and* your feelings were in line. In fact, you may have found that people stopped offering you sweets.

Or maybe you're trying to create a dream. And one day you get sick and tired of waiting for the right time and you decide to no longer allow the job market or the economy to determine your reality. You get out there and do whatever you need to do to create your desires. No matter what it takes! No matter how stupid or menial it may seem! And miracles just seem to appear.

You can have the most powerful thoughts for a project, but if your feelings do not match, little will happen. Even if we persist—forcing our dream to happen—the result seems to be nothing but struggle, struggle, and more struggle. For example, you can do all types of positive thinking affirmations to create more money, but if down in your heart you really feel that you *do not deserve* more money, you will not create it. If you manage to create an unexpected windfall of money, you find that you cannot hold onto your money or even enjoy it. Your thinking and your feelings are at war and, as Caroline Myss says,

> *"Whenever there is an issue between the heart and the mind, the heart will always win."*

Similarly, if you have basic feelings of undeservability, these feelings will prevent you from creating a more loving relationship. You may attend workshops and lectures on opening up to better relationships, but if you really do not feel that *you deserve* a relationship, you will always sabotage it. In their book, *Conscious Loving* by Gay and Kathryn Hendricks, they describe what they call the *upper limits problem*. This occurs when what we are experiencing in life exceeds what we feel we truly deserve. We hit our *upper limits*—the highest limit of happiness that we feel we deserve. And so, in order to get back to what feels *normal*, we create a problem or a fight.

Stav and I see this a lot with the couples we work with. As things get better, the couple may begin to experience more problems. We have seen one or both people hit their upper limits and then try to scale down the relationship to what feels comfortable. It may not be what they want, it may not be happy, but it is comfortable because it is familiar.

There is an old Arab tale that demonstrates how our feelings of anger, hate and unforgiveness create the hell in our lives. A man released a genie from a bottle and was granted only one wish. He could ask for anything in the world—the only catch was that his worst enemy would receive double. And so he thought of asking for gold, but then realized that his worst enemy would get twice as much gold. The same with camels, land, and wives. And this, the man would not allow. He stayed awake at nights, his hatred burning within, trying to find a way to win without his enemy benefiting from his wish.

Finally, one day, in true ego fashion, the man made his wish. He wished to be made blind in one eye.

How many of us, when it comes to creating our reality, would rather hurt ourselves than let our enemy (or partner) get the upper hand? How many divorces bankrupt years of savings in order to be sure that the other person does not win? This is the role that feelings play in creating our reality.

Jesus says in *A Course in Miracles* that,

> *Thought and belief combine into a power surge that can literally move mountains.*

**Text Pg. 26 / 31**

Thoughts are the mental aspect of our being. Belief is the *feelings* we have around those thoughts.

Generally, the thinking part is easy. All it takes is the willingness to change our minds. We can inundate, cajole and bludgeon our minds into submission, and soon our thoughts begin to follow in the new direction. It's like driving a herd of cattle. Change one thought and others tend to follow.

But changing our feelings is a bit trickier. It's like trying to drive a herd of cats. None of them listens. They each resist any attempt at control and wander at will. You cannot force a feeling to be anything other than what it is. You cannot control a feeling. All you can do is suppress it (which leads to more problems) or express it. The trick is learning how to express it responsibly and lovingly, without hurting yourself or others. In other words, without creating more hell!

Admittedly, feelings are messy. If you are angry about something, you can deny the anger, you can pretend that it doesn't bother you, but you will **still be angry**. The anger may go underground for awhile but ultimately it will seep out, whether you like it or not, tainting and messing up all your wonderful plans.

Truly creating your reality requires that you become conscious of both your thoughts and feelings and then finding a balance between them. Feelings are the "glue" that keeps our unconscious thoughts from changing. Too much thinking leads to logical, reasonable, safe, conservative, "dead" people because they live in their heads and are dissociated from their feelings. They may accomplish goals through the force of their wills, but there is no joy in the accomplishment, no sense of peace. Conversely, too much feeling leads to over-reactive, impulsive people who rush around without direction, jumping from relationship to relationship, from job to job, accomplishing little and feeling increasingly frustrated.

So what do we do with these feelings? There are lots of people who can help in teaching you to identify and release your feelings, and this book will not go into that subject. My personal method is to have a session of Breath Integration. But one of the quickest ways I have learned to release a negative feeling is to surrender to it *without acting on it*. That means that if you realize that deep down inside you have deep feelings of hate towards someone, you allow the feeling to rise. You breathe into it and give it life. Let the emotions overwhelm you, but do not act on them. Do not call the person in question and read them the riot act. Do not attack and do not blame. Attack increases guilt—another feeling that ultimately keeps us from feeling at all.

When you allow the negative feelings to come up, you will find that after awhile, they dissipate. It's as if all they wanted was to be acknowledged.

The following is a wonderful quote I read in Frank Herbert's *Dune*. Whenever the hero experienced fear, he would repeat to himself:

> *I must not fear. Fear is the mind-killer. Fear is the little death that brings total obliteration. I will face my fear. I will permit it to pass over me and through me. And when it has gone past I will turn the inner eye to see its path. Where the fear has gone there will be nothing. Only I will remain.*

When you begin to acknowledge and release any negative feelings you then leave room for the feeling of love. **Any feeling, deeply felt *without blame*, always leads to love**. And love is the one emotion that will lead us to our dreams, our perfect relationships and back to ourselves.

## Choosing to be Right or Happy

Changing our minds can be the most challenging experience we encounter, because we all like to be right (it *feels* better). We don't like to see where we may be mistaken or how we may have a part in our own problems. *A Course in Miracles* has a powerful statement, which I use whenever I'm at the crossroads in my mind.

> *Do you prefer that you be right or happy?*
>
> **Text pg. 573 / 617**

The desire to be right will kill a relationship more quickly than anything. Since the purpose of relationships is to heal (i.e., to grow and expand), insisting on being right prevents us from seeing the part we play in generating the very things we fear and, therefore, prevents us from growing.

If I have a thought that, "Women are not dependable and they always leave me," then until I work and change that thought, I will continue to have relationships with women who leave me. In fact, I will actually only be attracted to women who will leave me. Why? Because at a subconscious level, this is *my reality* around women, and subconsciously I want to be right! I will not be attracted to women who will stay, because then I would be wrong about women and I would have to change my mind. However, in order to change my mind, it would take self-reflection, awareness and some honest truth telling. It would take some discipline and work. It would take—a miracle—a change in my perception. If I am too frightened or lazy to change, it is easier to blame the world than to actually do something about it. And if, by chance, I do attract a woman who wants to stay, and I don't change my mind, I will create the problem myself in order to be right.

For example, if I persist in believing that women leave me, but I am in a relationship with someone who will not leave, I will test her to see if she will leave. At some level I truly do not *feel* that this is genuine. My fears of abandonment will come up and I'll begin to question her whereabouts, who she had lunch with, whether she really had a flat tire that night, etc. If she's late, I'll wonder what she was really doing. I'll begin to smother her, bug her, and test her. And after awhile what do you think she will want to do? Leave! Once again, I get to be right but unhappy.

Ask yourself how many times you have tested a relationship just to see whether that person matches a thought you had. Did you ever say something, just to see the other person's reaction? Did you ever test someone to the point where they threw up their hands in frustration and screamed, "I just can't do it right for you! I can never win with you!"? And then did you secretly smirk with the thought that "I knew he/she wasn't that perfect. I knew he/she couldn't really put up with me!"? When we realize that we are indeed testing our partner, we may initially feel ashamed or resistant to open to the truth. But if we let down our guard, just a little, we begin to see the part we play in all of our problems. And you know what? It's not that bad.

We can't run away from our mind's creative power. We do not have a choice in whether we create or not create. The only choice we have is in **what** we create. Many people think that if they just change their surroundings, get a new job, a new relationship or if they move across the country, then things will be different. The problem is that they still take their minds with them, and the thoughts that created the original problems will create the same thing again.

In the movie *Pretty Woman*, Julia Roberts plays the part of a prostitute who is falling in love with Richard Gere, her customer. She feels bad about what she's done with her life and has a lot of self-hate. At one point, he offers to set her up in her own apartment and pay for her expenses.

"What good would that do?" she asks.

"Well, it would get you off the street," he replies.

"That's just geography," she retorts.

She knows, deep inside, that changing her address will change nothing until she changes within. So, too, it is with us.

When we begin to realize that it is our own thoughts that create the world we see, the realization forces us to begin to be responsible for our lives. No matter how comforting it may *seem*, blaming our parents, society, or our teachers no longer works, because we have to acknowledge that *we are the ones responsible* for our own reality. Throughout our lives we have been exposed to many teachings from our parents, teachers, other adults and our peers. Some of those teachings were correct, but some \ guided or just plain wrong. If we cannot seem to create th relationship, it is not because we were told by others that we were unlovable. It is because we *truly believed* that we were unlovable and then we took on the belief as truth. Those other people were merely a reflection of what we already unconsciously believed. You see, our experiences do not create our beliefs, but the other way around. Our beliefs create the experiences in our lives that thereby reinforce our beliefs.

But at some point we have to take charge of our beliefs. Hanging onto the past and blaming our teachers for not being perfect gets us nowhere. We are never the victims of our past. We are only the victims of our present conscious and unconscious thoughts. The good news, though, is that we can choose to change our current thoughts, thereby changing our current situation.

Les Brown, the inspirational and motivational speaker, was judged to be "educable mentally retarded" when he was a child. But at some point, along with the support and love of significant people in his life, he chose to change that perception. He decided to believe and act differently. And through the years he has built a multi-million dollar speaking and teaching company that inspires the world.

Becoming responsible for your thoughts and feelings is at first frightening, but ultimately freeing. Frightening because it looks as if it's a big job to track down and change our erroneous thoughts. Freeing because now we know that there is nobody holding us back, except our own thoughts and pride. We've been using our powerful, unlimited minds trying to control others, trying to prove facts that aren't true and trying to boost up our fragile, little egos. We use the nuclear reactors of our minds to play video games instead of powering and enriching the world! When we begin to channel our thoughts and harness them to the force of our feelings, then we begin to see how truly powerful we are.

# Self Discovery Quiz

- *Do you spend a lot of time worrying? About what? Does worrying take you any closer to solving your problems?*

- *If you think about your problems all the time, and our thoughts create all the time, what do you think you are creating more of?*

- *Since thoughts always create at some level, is it possible to successfully hide your secret thoughts, shame or guilt from your partner?*

- *What thoughts would you be most ashamed of having another person find out? How can you release the energy spent on these thoughts so they no longer run you?*

- *If you persist in having negative, critical self-talk, what do you think you will create daily in the world out there?*

- *Do you have any resistance to the idea that your parents have absolutely nothing to do with your current life, that your life is based on all your present thoughts of what you think your life should be?*

- *Who planted the thoughts in your mind that you need to change? Are you willing to forgive those people for their mistakes and change your mind?*

- *Are you willing to forgive yourself for embracing those thoughts?*

*To reach the port of heaven, we must sail,*
*sometimes with the wind*
*and sometimes against it —*
*but we must sail, not drift or lie at anchor.*
Oliver Wendell Holmes, Sr.

*Religion is for people who are afraid of hell.*
*Spirituality is for people who have been there.*
Anonymous

*In three words I can sum up everything*
*I've learned about life.*
*It goes on.*
Robert Frost

*If you would discover new lands,*
*you must first consent*
*to lose sight of the shore.*
Andre Gidé

# Law #2:
# "Love Brings Up Everything Unlike Itself"

Have you ever noticed that after the "honeymoon" period of a relationship, we begin to get irritated with our partner for any reason whatsoever? Ever noticed how after the initial ecstasy of love, we begin to feel fearful about losing this person, or fearful about what they may see if they really saw who we are, or fearful about who they may really be? Have you ever noticed that the very things that attracted you to this person now irritate you? What happens that changes that initial flood of lust and love into judgments and fear?

Remember that the true purpose of a relationship is to heal— to grow and expand as a person. One of the ways we create the stage for healing is by repeating and hopefully healing our childhood wounds, our forgotten hurts and pain. When we commit to a path of action, such as love, anything that is in the way of reaching that goal must come up. In this way, it can then become conscious, be addressed and finally released. Many of us unconsciously have a fear of future hurts commingled with the memories of our old hurts.

Being in the presence of love is like turning on a light in a messy room. Before the light was on, we were comfortable, thinking our world was just fine and dandy. But then the light is turned on and illuminates all the areas that need to be changed, and this throws us into confusion, fear and possibly low self-esteem. We see all the dust, cobwebs and boxes in disarray and we blame the light for causing all this upset. But it's not the light that's the problem. It's our hidden emotional clutter that was *already there* that's the problem.

How does healing come about in a relationship? Healing occurs when we begin to face and accept the parts of ourselves that have been hurt, judged and suppressed. Have you ever noticed that an intellectual man may fall in love with a very emotional woman and then judge her for being too emotional? Or an artist falls in love with an athlete and then judges him for not being able to be more expressive? Why are these people attracted to each other in the first place? Why doesn't the intellectual stick with other intellectuals, and the artist only date other creative people?

The reason is simple. It is because the people we are attracted to are expressing certain characteristics that **we** have suppressed and unconsciously wish to experience for ourselves. These are characteristics that we suppressed as children because we thought that was what we needed to do in order to be accepted and survive psychologically in our family. The intellectual person wants to feel more, but feels threatened when emotions come up. So he feels his feelings through his wife, and then judges her for being so emotional. He defends himself from taking any responsibility for the possibility that maybe he, too, wants to feel. But the love in a relationship gives us the opportunity to heal and become whole, once these suppressed traits are activated, accepted, and loved.

Let me give you an example. Let's suppose that a loving, fulfilled, well-rounded person has the following six traits (these are by no means all of the traits):

- **Intelligent** – the ability to think, plan and use logic.
- **Emotional** – the ability to let oneself feel, regardless if the feeling is negative or positive.
- **Sensual** – the ability to enjoy the senses—to smell a rose, to enjoy a loving caress, to give or receive a massage.
- **Creative** – the ability to visualize new answers and methods and to express oneself in his/her own unique way.

- **Athletic** – the ability to move the body, play, run and jump.
- **Sexual** – the ability to enjoy the sexual aspect
  of his/her body.

A model of this balanced person might look like this:

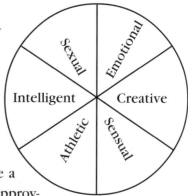

Now let's look at Bill. He grew up in a family that shamed him when he cried or had any feelings at all. "You're such a baby!" they said. "Be a man! Stop your whimpering." Maybe he liked playing with watercolors and was told that "only sissies paint."

Now remember when you are a child, the thought of your family disapproving of you *feels* like a death sentence. The threat that the love and caring will be taken away (no matter how little love there may be) means that you will be on your own—that there will be no one to take care of you—that you will die. This is how we *feel* as children. And so, in order to survive in his family, Bill suppresses his feelings and his creativity and concentrates on developing his intelligence and athletic ability. When feelings come up, he tries to rationalize (*rational lies*) or think the feeling away. He learns how to be sexual but has little sensuality. And at some level, he now feels incomplete.

His model looks like this:

Now Jane was raised in a family that told her that girls were not smart and couldn't play sports. In order for her to survive, she suppressed her natural intellectual and athletic abilities. Her father was not a loving man, and she yearns to be loved and understood. She has no trouble feeling; in fact, she can emote at the drop of a hat! She has a hard time making decisions because she sees and feels all sides of an issue without enough balance from her intellectual side. Since she suppresses her athletic ability, she judges her body, how it moves and acts, and has a hard time enjoying sex. She, too, feels incomplete. Her model looks like this:

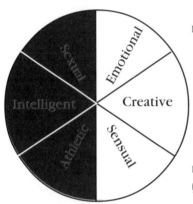

And then one day, their eyes meet rom across a dance floor, and *ZING!* something inside them stirs. There is a kindred feeling that "here is someone who can now complete me." Bill is attracted to this feeling, creative woman, and she is attracted to this intelligent, athletic man. What they think is *love at first bt* is actually the siren call of their unresolved issues with their families—it is the unconscious call to reawaken their suppressed characteristics. They get into a relationship and, for a while, they are in heaven.

But after some time, they begin to get on each other's nerves. "Whenever I ask her what she *thinks* about something, she always tells me how she *feels*," he complains. "She gushes about anything! It's just aggravating!" And she may complain, "He's always *doing* something. It's Go! Go! Go! Why can't he just sit and talk? He only wants to have sex but not to relate."

What is happening at this point is that the couple fights and judges each other for the very aspects that they fell in love with. If this continues, the relationship may break up or both sides may just shut down. Either way, the love gets lost and each person once again feels incomplete.

You see, the suppressed aspects of each person are now getting activated; they are trying to come alive. But for Bill to allow his feelings to come out means death to the *little child* within him, and so he defends against letting his feelings out. The same is true for Jane. When Bill asks her what she thinks about an issue, she reverts to feelings, because that is safer than thinking.

What we have here is a classic example of a special relationship. Each person sees his or her partner as having something that will fill the dark hole within. They are trying to **get** something from their partner in order to feel complete. But there is nothing to *get*. Each person already has those qualities—they have just not been activated and honored.

The only way out of this situation is to begin to see that each person has aspects that can help heal the other. This is where a special relationship can transform into a holy relationship by changing the purpose from *getting* to *sharing*—from judging differences to empowering each other. In this way we learn to love and accept the parts we judged and suppressed.

Jane can now teach Bill that it is safe to feel, to open to creativity and to enjoy the sensual side of life. And Bill can now teach Jane how to enjoy her body and how to balance her emotions with thinking. In this way, they begin to heal the wounds from their childhood and become whole people once again. However, to paraphrase Harville Hendricks,

"In order to heal, the very act that will heal both people will be the act **least** likely to be done."

When Stav or I are working with a couple, a very common technique we have couples use is to hold each other. What this involves is simply taking turns holding your partner for an agreed upon amount of time. The one doing the holding is the "giver" and their job is to emotionally and psychically support their partner. The one being held is the "receiver" and their job is to just receive the other person's love. The receiver does not even hold the giver back but just lies in his/her arms—receiving.

This is done without talking. Many times when we feel uncomfortable, what we try to do is to "talk the feelings away." We get busy relating "how silly" this feels, or how it reminds us of something from the past. In this way we prevent ourselves from just experiencing the feeling. So just *notice* your feelings and remember to take deep breaths—both of you.

Notice how it feels to be the "giver." Are there any feelings of resentment? Any feelings of always having to be the "strong one?" Does it remind you of being a child and always having to take care of somebody else? Does it feel good to have your love received without you really having to do anything else?

Notice how it feels to be the "receiver." Are there any feelings of shame or guilt around receiving this person's love and attention? Do you feel needy? Do you feel that you want to push this person away because they are getting too close? Does it feel good? Does it feel like finally you can just be loved without doing anything?

After the allotted period of time, switch positions, so that the "giver" becomes the "receiver." Later, if you chose, you can talk about the experience and any feelings or insights that may have occurred.

Using this technique, Bill allows himself to learn about feelings. He holds Jane as she is crying over something, and he notices he feels uncomfortable. He may even judge her or himself, but he just *notices* the judgments without getting attached. He lets it be OK that he feels uncomfortable. That is because he now knows that the uncomfortable feeling is just his defenses getting activated. It's just his fears. He lets the uncomfortable feeling grow and grow until one day, he too begins to cry. Jane responds not with criticism (which he unconsciously expects), but with love and acceptance. She sees him as a courageous, powerful, loving man—not the wimp he thought he had to protect. And as he allows more of his feelings to surface, as he learns how to use and express them responsibly, he balances his personality.

So, too, it goes with Jane. As she allows herself to trust her intelligence and take action, balanced with her feelings, she sees that she, too, can heal.

When I began working on improving myself, I remember learning how I should not judge, because that is one of the many ways the ego uses to keep people separate. But the more I tried **not** to judge, the more judgmental I began to feel. I felt as if I were judging everybody for anything I could think of. Or, the more loving and accepting I tried to become, the more separate and angry I felt. I realized that these judgments and unloving thoughts were how I lived *every moment of my day*. I was an unloving judgment machine. At first I was tempted to think that non-judgments or acceptance did not work. Then I was reminded that *"Love brings up everything unlike itself."* The love did not make me feel more judgmental, it merely illuminated **all** of my judgmental thoughts that were already there, the conscious and the unconscious judgments.

Relationships are powerful healing tools because they are mirrors that reflect our inner thoughts and feelings back to our awareness. They shine a light into our inner selves, exposing the secrets and fears which we prefer to ignore, although these fears continually hurt us. In the presence of love, our Divine side brings up our hurts and fears in an effort to relieve the pain of the past and to see the present with new eyes.

When we remember this law, it makes it easier to resist the desire to blame our partner for the feelings we are having. You see, nobody can make you feel anything unless that feeling is already within you. Nobody can make you feel angry unless there is already suppressed anger that needs to be expressed. Nobody can make you feel sad unless there is sadness that needs to be released.

According to *A Course in Miracles*, our job is not to seek out love, but to seek out all of our barriers to receiving love. We need to go deep into our egos and face and feel everything we believe is unlovable about us. Only by facing, embracing and finally loving and accepting every part of ourselves can we find peace and wholeness. So instead of blaming others for how we feel, we begin to love and accept those very feelings we are running from. We begin to love and accept those very aspects of ourselves that we have been running from.

For many of us, love brings up our basic neediness. Nobody likes to feel needy, especially nowadays with all the talk about codependency. But neediness is a basic human trait. We all start out needy; as babies we needed another person to support and provide for us. But somehow the world makes it wrong to be needy. We are told to "Grow up!", "Get a life!" and "Take care of others and forget your needs." So we get a stiff upper lip, suppress the tears and never let another person know what we want or need. And we feel empty. And when we feel empty, we tend to whine, blame and feel resentful towards everybody else who gets their way. As you can see, this is merely more hell on the way.

Throughout life there will be many times when we feel needy—losing a job, or a relationship, writing a book, opening a store, getting married, going for our dream, or just plain feeling lonely. The problem arises when, instead of acknowledging the neediness, instead of letting ourselves *feel* vulnerable and needy, we try to **trick** and manipulate somebody into giving us the love we crave. And all we end up with is feeling guilty for manipulating, and the other person feeling angry because they are being used. Ultimately, our partner runs away (physically or emotionally) because we are not owning our own neediness.

Bob Mandel, in his book, *Open Heart Therapy*, tells about a time when he was feeling especially needy around his wife. Being a therapist, he initially thought that this was a bad feeling, and so for a while he attempted to suppress it. But the more he tried, the more needy he felt. He was so afraid to tell his wife how much he needed her, because then she might think he was codependent and leave him. But after a few days, he decided to face his fear and one morning, he turned to her in the kitchen and said,

"Sometimes I think I would die if I didn't have you in my life. I need you."

She turned to him, smiled and replied,

"I know. Sometimes I feel that way too."

Once Bob acknowledged the neediness, the needy feelings left, and he got to see that wanting and needing his wife wasn't bad or weak. It was another part of the emotional spectrum. Sharing his neediness with his wife helped him to feel closer to her.

Once, during my practitioner training, the class was discussing and processing sexual issues. I began to feel uneasy and shameful. It took me a while to realize that I was embarrassed about a particular sexual thought that I sometimes had. It was a thought I felt was certainly perverted. Although the love and the acceptance in the room were allowing me to bring up my sexual issues in order for me to heal, it also brought up my fear.

I hung onto my fear for awhile then finally decided to face my fear of rejection and divulged to the group my secret, sexual thought. I expressed how it both attracted me and disgusted me. When I was finished, I looked around the class, feeling like a pervert, waiting for rejection. Joe, our teacher, spoke.

"Okay, so how many people in this room have that same fantasy or thought? Raise your hands."

Just about every person in the class, *my ex-girlfriend included*, raised their hand. At first my ego had the thought,

"Wow, there's a lot of perverts here!"

But then I stopped thinking and *looked* at my classmates. They too had their little bits of fear but they were all loving me and I saw love in their eyes as they acknowledged the courage it took to share my fears. I got to see in that moment that I wasn't special or perverted. There were others who thought like me, hid secrets like me and suffered like me. My sharing started other people sharing their secret shames and guilt. The day ended with a great sense of innocence for ourselves, our bodies and our sexuality.

Love brings up everything unlike itself, because we want to heal, to be whole, to once again feel our innocence. When we stop blaming our partner and others for the feelings that arise in us and experience the feelings that need to be released, then we have an opportunity to experience our innocence.

The important thing is not to get scared and run away and give up, but to push through the *seeming* insurmountable obstacles or differences. Allow the light to stay on so you can clean up the messy room of your psyche. Tidy up and bring illumination and order to the random, chaotic reactivity of your past programming. Then and only then will you become more intentional in how you treat yourself and your relationship.

The final goal is love. As we remind ourselves that "love does bring up everything unlike itself," it gives us courage to try a little longer. It reassures us that we are on the right track. The feelings of surrender and connection we experience once we push through our fears and judgements remind us that only love is real.

# Affirmations

- *As I heal, I find it easier and easier to feel.*
- *As I feel, I find it easier and easier to heal.*
- *My sense of pride is no longer a good enough reason not to change.*
- *Anything between me and my partner is also between me and God.*
- *Anything that is between me and God I now allow to come up and be healed.*
- *I have **never** sinned. I have made mistakes, and those can be corrected.*
- *I no longer have anything to hide from God or myself.*
- *I now trust God in me to only bring up the lessons that I can truly handle.*
- *I am in no hurry to heal. I take one step at a time, knowing that each step takes me closer to God.*
- *Since I have nothing to hide from God, I also have nothing to hide from my partner.*

*When I was a boy of fourteen,*
*my father was so ignorant*
*I could hardly stand to have the old man around.*
*But when I got to be twenty-one,*
*I was astonished at how much the old man had*
*learned in seven years.*

**Mark Twain**

*When my mother complained that I was a*
*procrastinator, I told her, "Just you wait."*

**Judy Tenuta**

*Sixty years ago I knew everything;*
*now I know nothing;*
*education is a progressive discovery*
*of our own ignorance.*

**Will Durant**

"I THINK THE PROBLEM IS THEY'VE BEEN PARENTS FOR ONLY SIX YEARS WHILE WE'VE BEEN KIDS ALL OUR LIVES."

© 1999 Reprinted courtesy of Bunny Hoest and King Features

# Law #3:
# "Anything Unresolved With My Parents Will Recur in My Relationships"

W hen I was in therapy during a previous marriage and complaining once again about my wife, my therapist would ask me,

"So, what was your relationship with your mother like when you were growing up?"

I remember asking my therapist what my mother had to do with my current relationship. I remember feeling that this *idiot* psychiatrist was just trying to use some psychiatric mumbo-jumbo on me. The problem had nothing to do with my mother! The problem was with my wife!

Years later, after another divorce, as I began to follow the trail of my feelings into my heart, I found my mother waiting for me. I finally began to realize that she had been in every relationship I ever had. Not my physical mother, but the mother I **thought** I had. The mother I thought that didn't understand me. The mother I thought that didn't love me the way I wanted to be loved. Since I saw my mother a certain way, I expected women to be that way too. I found myself only attracted to women who fit my unconscious expectations. I subconsciously expected every woman to be like my mother, and I got to be right.

In an effort to heal, we will be attracted to people who have qualities of our caregivers (this includes babysitters, teachers, coaches, bosses, etc.) Initially it may be with the parent with whom we have the most unfinished business. Over time, it may be a combination of the two. As we see our parents, we also see others. As we see our parents, we also project those attributes onto any other authority figure, God included. The way I saw my mother was the way I saw all women. I saw conflict and misunderstanding, I expected conflict and misunderstanding and I got conflict and misunderstanding. But what was really scary was that the very things I judged my mother for, I also did myself. And I caused the same type of pain in others.

Our parents were the first people from whom we learned about relationships. They helped develop the "blueprint" of how we relate to ourselves and the world. And from that place we project onto our intimate partners our idea of men, women and authority figures.

The way they treated us taught us how to treat ourselves. The way they treated each other and the way they treated our brothers and sisters taught us how to relate to others. If they suppressed their feelings and were afraid to express their love, we learned that love should never be expressed. If we saw people who used and abused love in order to control others, we learned to never trust love. If they didn't hold us enough or give us positive feedback, we learned that we were unlovable and that there was something wrong with us. If secrets were common in our family, we learned to be secretive and to not trust that others are telling us the truth. If screaming, name-calling and abuse were rampant, we may have related to others similarly or withdrew. If we were happy, having fun and skipping through the house and they screamed at us for being too loud and always underfoot, we learned to suppress our joy and aliveness.

If our parents were open and loving, if they taught us how to handle difficulty and differences of opinion with love, we will tend to relate to the world the same way.

Trying to run away from the issues solves nothing. In fact, though we may feel that we have escaped, we may still be acting under our parents' rules. I am reminded of a story of a little six-year-old boy, who was sitting angrily on a curb. A man, seeing the boy, asked,

"What are you doing, son?"

"I'm running away from home," replied the child.

"Then why are you just sitting here?'

"Because my mom told me never to cross the street."

You may *act* differently when you grow up ("I'll never be like Dad"), but if you do not release the emotions that tie you to your father, you will still end up acting out the effects of your relationship with him. A person who was beaten and controlled by his father may have learned to suppress his anger. He may put up a front of the "nice guy," letting other people get their way, because he doesn't want to be a tyrant like his dad. He may then feel "justified" that he never acts like his dad, but he will still feel beaten down and controlled by others.

In addition, the suppressed anger at not expressing his needs adds to his old anger at his father, and it just grows and grows. Unexpressed anger *always* seeps out—the anger must go somewhere. But since he doesn't allow himself to get angry (that would be like Dad), he may become controlling and manipulative. He may express his anger unconsciously through passive-aggressive acts such as "forgetting" important dates, chronically being late, being judgmental or just tuning people out. And though he may not be aware of it, whenever he controls another to get his way, he will unconsciously feel guilty for being like his dad (controlling). And as his relationships catch on to his control, they will get angry and begin to fight back. And more and more, his life will look like his life with his dad.

Even if he takes the opposite route, becoming just as abusive and violent as his dad in an effort to keep the world from hurting him, he will then feel just like dad *all the time*. In either case, Dad is still very much alive in his life.

If your dad was stingy, you may spend money on others, even when you don't have it, in an effort to show how generous (and unlike Dad) you are. But this does not work because, after awhile, you will begin to feel that people only love you for your money. As a result, you may become resentful, hold back your love (money) and act out your resentment in other ways. And in holding back your money, you will look stingy—just like your dad. Or maybe you are generous with others but not with yourself (because you can't afford it), and now you are treating yourself as Dad treated you.

You see, when we *try* to act differently, at the effect of our parent's behavior, we are not being **who we are**, we are being Not-Dad, Not-Mom, or Anti-Dad, Anti-Mom. In order to become who we truly are, we need to become more conscious of our intentions and reactivity. We need to understand what drives us. This means being and acting the way that is right for us *in the moment*, whether it reminds us of our parents or not. *This means that there will be times that we will feel as if we are just like our parents.*

In the example of the stingy father, you can see that acting the opposite and extravagantly spending money isn't the answer. Neither is watching every penny. We have to find a balanced perspective in each situation. There may come a time when your child is asking you to buy him/her something that you *know* if you did, it would not serve the family. And you'll have to say, No." At that moment, even though it may be the correct answer, you will feel like you are your dad.

So if acting differently does not solve the problem, what does? For example, have you ever noticed what happens when somebody tries to stop a habit, such as overeating, because it's *good* for them or because others disapprove? If the person isn't doing it for him/herself, he/she will resist and probably react with anger in covert ways. Or he/she may even pick up new habits, such as exercising too much, nail biting, maybe even smoking. This is because the *basic thoughts and feelings* that drove that person to overeat in the first place have not been addressed. All that has changed is their behavior, but the old thought pattern is still in place.

When people are badgered or threatened into changing against their will, there is usually anger and resistance. What I tell people who want to lose weight, stop smoking or break a habit is to first love and accept themselves as a smoker or an overweight person. Then I ask them to start exploring the reasons that drove them to smoke or overeat in the first place. Was it peer pressure, a need to look "cool," a way to numb out emotional pain? Behind every compulsion, there are hidden feelings of shame and fear. This pain needs to be expressed and released before the habit can be addressed. Embracing the negative aspects of our psyche is the first step in letting go of a negative habit. Then, from a place of self-love, the person can choose the path he/she wants to follow.

When I have a disagreement with Stav and she reminds me of my mother, I *initially* react in my old ways. I treat Stav *as if* she is my mother. You see, as a child I was very obstinate. Life with me was a battle of wills, and though my mother was bigger than I was, I always found ways to get even. Even though my mother would ask me what I wanted or how I wanted to be treated, I remember being so angry and bratty, that I would not tell her, even though I would have benefited.

And so, years later, even after years of training and learning, I *still* react in that old way at times. The difference is that now I am aware of my old reactions, or Stav can remind me. So, too, there are times that Stav reacts to me as if I were her father.

We have both learned over the years, though, to listen to each other and to back off from the reacting. Instead of being obstinate and unwilling to listen, I take a breath, remind myself that this is not my mother, and I listen, as best I can, to what she is saying. I have learned that my wife (and my mother) do not want to hurt or control me. They are both *very willing* to listen to my wants and needs, and I have also learned that it is safe to tell them.

Sometimes the Universe helps us to change our thoughts in sneaky ways. I have a wonderful friend who told me her story about an incident that helped increase her trust and love with her father and men in general. Her dad and many of the men in her life disappointed and hurt her, and so for a long time, she wouldn't trust men. As she became more and more interested in raising her spiritual consciousness, she became more and more angry that there seemed to be no female spiritual teachers. It seemed to her that even God was male-dominated. And so, for awhile, she rejected God and any religious teachings.

Then one day she saw a book about a spiritual teacher. On the cover was the photograph of a gentle looking woman. The title of the book was *Autobiography of a Yogi* by Paramahansa Yogananda. Now Yogananda was a man, but because of the Indian name, his long, beautiful hair and his gentle looks, she didn't realize that he was male until she was more than halfway through the book. By then she had developed a great love and respect for the writer, and his gender no longer mattered.

"I spent years running away from male teachers and when I finally thought I had found a female guru, she turned out to be a man," she told me with a twinkle in her eye. Since then, she has been able to see men with gentler eyes, **and** she has also found powerful female teachers.

An episode on the television show *Taxi* illustrates how crazy we are when we try to reject our parents and that, maybe, there were valid reasons for their rules. One day Jim, the burned-out ex-druggie, takes in a boy who runs away from home because he hates his parents and all their rules. They arrive at Jim's place, which is a large, converted warehouse.

"This is my place," says Jim. "At my place, I got no rules. You can do anything you want."

"No rules?"

"Nah! When I was growing up, my ma would never let me do things I wanted to do, like throwing a ball in the house. I hated those stupid rules."

"Yeah, my parents are the same. They never let me have any fun."

"Well, kiddo, you can do anything you want around here." Jim motions to a baseball sitting on the coffee table. "You can even throw that ball if you want."

"Really?"

"Sure, kid. Go ahead. Throw it."

The boy picks up the ball and throws it. It careens off a wall, knocks a lamp off the table and shatters a window. Jim's eyes suddenly light up in enlightenment.

"Maybe *that's* why my mother didn't want me throwing the ball in the house."

There were many things our parents did that were wrong. They made many mistakes. There were many things they did just because their parents did it. However, there were many things they did that were right. Our job, as adults, is to see our parents with compassion and to accept the rules, proverbs and sayings that resonate in us and leave behind what does not. We do not have to repeat the same mistakes our parents did, but we can also learn from their experience.

As I began to unfold and became more real about who I was, I had to start taking responsibility for *my part* in my relationship with my parents. Yes, they were wrong and did unwise things at times. However, I have found that as an adult I, too, am wrong and unwise at times. When I apologize for my mistakes, I remember the times my mom or dad apologized for their actions. I begin to have compassion for who they were—imperfect, growing people who were doing the best they could.

I think it was the Dalai Lama who was once asked how he saw Hitler. He replied, "I see him as a Child of God who still exhibits *unskilled behavior.*"

As we heal our relationships with our parents or as we become parents ourselves, we will create opportunities to see through their eyes, to feel what they felt and hopefully to understand them. We begin to see our parents as imperfect people with a lot of misguided, unskilled ways of living life. We get to complete the circle with them.

As we learn to understand them, we begin to feel compassion for them.

And as we learn about us, we begin to feel compassion for ourselves.

We may actually begin to feel a sense of connection as we realize the parts we played along with our parents.

We may even begin to see the threads of pain, life and love that weave their way throughout generations.

And with the compassion and connection come peace.

We find that the effects from Mom and Dad and our childhood wounds no longer control our lives. This leads to having deeper, more intimate relationships with others. And it is this mature, real love that feeds our soul.

# Affirmations

- *I now find it easier and easier to acknowledge what my parents did that was right and to release what was wrong. It does not serve me to hold onto my pain and suffering.*

- *I no longer expect my parents to be perfect.*

  *I no longer wait for my parents to grow up. I now take responsibility for my life and change it accordingly.*

- *The only one that needs to "grow up" is me.*

- *I no longer wait for my parents to say, "I'm sorry." I now apologize to myself and others for my misdeeds and correct any errors.*

- *I no longer blame my parents for what they taught me. I now take responsibility for choosing to hang onto those thoughts myself. Nobody can force me to believe anything! I now choose new thoughts!*

- *I now stop making my partner pay for my parent's mistakes.*

- *I now allow anything unresolved with my parents to be healed in my current relationships. I now also give myself permission to remember this affirmation.*

- *Nobody needs to pay anymore for my past hurts.*

- *I no longer project on my partner my unresolved issues with my parents.*

*We learn from experience.*
*A man never wakes up his second baby*
*just to see it smile.*

**Grace Williams**


*Those who cannot remember the past*
*are condemned to repeat it.*

**George Santayana**


*I don't know the key to success,*
*but the key to failure*
*is trying to please everybody.*

**Bill Cosby**


*Where there is an open mind,*
*there will always be a frontier.*

**Charles F. Kettering**

## Law #4:
# *"Lessons Will Be Repeated Until They are Learned"*

After you've been in a few relationships, if you're alert, you'll probably begin to see patterns emerging. You find yourself, for example, always attracted to the same type of woman or man, or you always end up in an abusive relationship. Even when we try to act the opposite, or select someone totally different, we still somehow end up with the same pattern.

If we've been abused, we may erect defenses to protect ourselves and decide never to let the abuse happen again, but in defending ourselves we may become abusive in an attempt to prevent another person from taking advantage of us.

For example, I've known women who felt that men were either controlling dictators or wimps, never realizing their role in the part they play. Let's take a woman who was raised by an abusive, controlling father. Unless she heals her issues with her father, she will actually be attracted to men who are abusive.

Why would she be attracted to someone like her father? Well, for starters, someone like her father would be *familiar*. These are her old, subconscious expectations. And since love, as shown by her father, was the only love she experienced, she will think, at some level, that that is what love looks like. Also, her unhealed issues with her father will unconsciously compel her to get into relationships with someone like him, in order to heal this representation of her father. If she can get love from this man, it will be like getting love from her father.

Now remember, just because the package looks different, this does not mean that the contents are different. Maybe the woman's father was physically abusive. She may be smart enough to avoid getting into a relationship with anyone who will hit her, but she may get into a relationship with someone who emotionally abuses her. Or someone who controls the finances. Or someone who lies and has affairs. All of these are forms of abuse.

She may wise up and say, "To hell with all this! I'm taking control from now on!"

She decides to never let another man take advantage of her, and so now she becomes the controller. She gets tough. She gets mean. She controls, dominates and in her own way becomes the abuser. But in defending and keeping men at arm's length, she doesn't allow herself to be vulnerable enough to receive a man's love. Once again, she feels that men just don't know how to love her. She begins to judge that her man is a wimp. She loses respect for him and ultimately she leaves, or he does. With this type of pattern, she can never win with men.

To break this vicious cycle of unsatisfying relationships, she will have to go back and *consciously* revisit her old wounds, which is a crucial step in forgiveness. There are feelings regarding her relationship with her father that need to be examined, felt, grieved and mourned. There is anger to be worked through.

She needs to forgive herself for believing that she doesn't deserve a loving man and for getting into abusive relationships in the first place. She also needs to start examining how her perceptions of men actually attract her to that type of person.

Though this process is usually perceived as painful, it is well worth the time and effort. The peace and the release of these old thoughts and feelings result in her being able to now consciously make healthier choices.

While there will always be controlling and abusive people, not all people are like that. As she clears out her own energy, as she cleans up any past garbage that fogs her perceptions, then her vision and intuition become sharper. She finds herself listening more and more to that inner voice that guides her and warns her if a certain person to whom she are attracted is "bad news." She sees more quickly the pattern that is emerging, and then she can choose to change or terminate the relationship if it's a dead end. And as she get clearer and clearer, she finds that this type of person is no longer in her life.

When we persist in hanging onto our false perceptions of people, we stifle our growth, because not only are we not growing and changing, but also our very perceptions will lead us to the people who will verify and affirm our judgments.

*A Course in Miracles* says,

> *Trials are but lessons that you failed to learn presented once again, so where you made a faulty choice before you now can make a better one, and thus escape all pain that what you chose before has brought you. In every difficulty ... Christ calls to you and gently says "My brother, choose again."*
>
> **Text pg. 619 / 666**

The process of Life is a constant series of fine tunings in our personal life. Lessons are repeated until we learn them. Then we get the next lesson. And we will never get a lesson that we are not ready to learn. When I was taking my spiritual trainings, I once told my teacher, Joe, about how I wanted a powerful woman in my life. "I want to create a powerful woman who can stand with me and share my life. I want a woman who will tell her truth and never sell out."

Joe looked at me with this smug look on his face and replied,

"Jerry, you couldn't handle a powerful woman. A powerful woman would eat you alive. There'd be nothing left but your glasses."

I was angry with him for saying that, but the real truth was that I was **not ready** for a powerful woman. I was much more interested in control and manipulation—in getting my way. I had too many hidden lies that I told myself. I was a wimp when it came to relating to a woman. What I really wanted was a woman I could control, a woman I could wrap around my little finger. Of course, once I got into such a relationship I would judge *her* for not being honest and powerful when in fact *it was I* who was not being honest and powerful.

It took a few more years of learning and self-discovery to finally create a powerful woman in my life. I had to practice telling the truth, even when I was afraid I would lose the relationship. I had to practice owning up to it when I was manipulating. I had to practice releasing any secret thoughts or judgments I had about women and myself. I had to practice admitting when I wanted to use guilt to control a woman. These years were well spent, preparing me for the relationship I have now.

The first day I saw Stav in church, I *knew* that she was the woman I had been searching for. Later, when she went into fear and judgment about me, I knew that her fears and judgments were not real, and I just continued loving her and expressing my truth. You see, she was looking for a truthful, powerful man in her life, and he had finally shown up. I had come far enough along not to believe her fears or judgments.

More importantly, I had learned to love myself more and to not believe *my own* fears and judgments about myself. Slowly, we developed the relationship we have today. We made lots of mistakes and we learned lots of lessons. We learned to say, "I'm sorry," to admit when we were wrong, to share our secret thoughts or judgments, to show our love, and to be the best friend and lover we can be. We are having more and more fun as our relationship continues to grow and evolve.

We *still* get upset when we have to repeat a lesson, but now we have tools and an experience of shared trust to take us through our ego thoughts. And we seem to be creating new lessons in areas we never dreamed of. As we heal our past relationships with others and continue to create a new kind of relationship together, we find that there is no problem that cannot be solved together.

The movie *Groundhog Day* is a good example of the value of repeating our lessons. It's about an obnoxious, narcissistic weatherman who one day goes into a sort of time warp in which he relives the same day over and over. He can change what he does during that day, but every morning, at six A.M., he wakes up in the same bed, listening to the same radio show, and it's Groundhog Day all over again. It doesn't matter if he commits crimes the night before and is caught by the police and thrown in jail, the next morning he wakes up safe in bed. It doesn't even matter whether he kills himself. The next morning, at six o'clock, there he is, safe in bed.

Since he can relive every day over, he decides to try to seduce the female producer of his news show. Each day he learns more and more about her, her likes and dislikes in order to get on her good side. But what happens (which is the same thing that happens to all of us) is that no matter how charming he *acts*, his basic control, manipulation and sliminess ooze out. In the last minute, she senses that something is wrong and rejects him every time.

Ultimately, he gets tired of the games, gives up, and begins to do the things he always thought he'd like to try. He learns to play piano, create ice sculptures, he reads the classics—after all, he has all the time in the world.

At one point, after seeing an old wino die in an alley, he begins to feel compassion and makes it a point to rescue the man. Every day he tries to save the man's life by getting to him earlier, feeding him, giving him money, but every night the man still dies. And the weatherman slowly begins to realize that some things just cannot be changed. But those that can be changed, he'll do something about.

The weatherman begins to care for people. He becomes a one-man crusader, doing good and helping others wherever he is needed. By working on himself and opening to others, he becomes a naturally wonderful person and, of course, in one of his repeating days, his producer begins to like him. It is through caring for others and developing compassion that he finally breaks the curse of repeating the same day, and his life proceeds on a much happier course.

We all live in a similar movie. The days may change, the scenery may change and the actors may change, but the same lesson is given to us until we learn it. When our heart begins to open and we begin to do the things we love to do, when we start caring about other people and we find joy and purpose in everything we do, then we become the person we are looking for. We are more fun to be with, and our curse (pattern) is broken. We stop making the same mistakes and we graduate to a new lesson. Of course, this will now be an opportunity to make *new mistakes*, but that's how we learn.

## Breaking the Pattern

So how do we break our patterns? By *consciously* going into them without losing ourselves in them. The reason a pattern is so persuasive is because there is an element of excitement in it. Take me, for example. I always seemed to be attracted to women who were *bad* for me. They were angry (at men), sexy, outspoken and outrageous. They excited me.

But whenever I got into a relationship with somebody who excited me, I would get so afraid of losing her that I would *do anything* to keep her around. I would sell out. I would spend money I couldn't afford. I wouldn't tell my truth for fear of losing her. I wouldn't ask for what I wanted for fear of seeming pushy. Slowly she (and I) would lose respect for the man with whom she fell in love. We would ultimately break up.

Then I tried getting into relationships with women who were *good* for me—women who were quiet, loving and sedate. But they didn't excite me. They loved me and I loved them the best I could, but the spark was not there! And I felt guilty for somehow using them.

And so I would leave—for another woman—a *bad* one. Back and forth I would go. Good, bad, good, bad. Now, don't get me wrong. *Neither* of these types of women was *good nor bad*. That was *my perception* of them. But my relationship life looked like an unending battle—the exciting (bad) women ate me alive, the unexciting (good) women bored me. I couldn't win and they couldn't win.

What I finally realized was this: the answer was *in the pattern* not running from it. And so I made myself a promise. I promised that I would only get into relationships with women who excited me, *and* I promised that I would **not sell out my soul**! I would become as honest and forthright as I could, even if it meant losing her love. This meant that I would be truthful.

As so, when I began new relationships with these promises, I would let myself feel my fear and then tell my truth anyway. I told her that I loved her. I told her I wanted her. I told her she was the most important person in my life.

I also told her what I didn't like. I told her what I judged. I told her what I wanted. I told her my faults. I made many mistakes and I learned to correct them. Over time I got better and better.

The analogy I give is that following your pattern in a relationship is like riding the edge of a hurricane. You can use the force and the excitement to stimulate and propel you, but as soon as you sell your soul to keep a relationship, you get sucked down the middle and lose it all.

Is my life with Stav like riding a hurricane? You bet it is! It is the most exciting, wonderful, exhilarating experience in my life. We have both learned the lessons of being sucked down the middle, and so we tell our truth, we risk the love, and, all the while, we have the time of our lives!

## *Life's Way of Correcting Mistakes*

You can't run away from your lessons. You can try to cheat by taking shortcuts, but Life always evens the score—gently at first, and more loudly as time goes on. When we get out of integrity, Life has a way of leading us back to correct the error.

When I was a senior in high school, I took trigonometry because it was a college preparation course (not because I wanted to, believe me!). I tried to understand it, but I could not grasp what the hell tangents, sines and cosines were. What good were they for, anyway? After a few weeks of struggling, I gave up. A girl who sat next to me in class let me cheat from her paper, and I barely passed with a "C". I felt bad about that class, but I felt there was nothing else I could do short of flunking. I needed to pass for college credit, and besides, I figured I would never use trigonometry anyway.

Many years later, I got interested in computers and I decided that I wanted to write some computer games. If you want to program a "shoot-em-up" game that tracks the angle of a bullet, guess what you need to know in order to calculate the path of that bullet? Trigonometry! I ended up going to a college bookstore and buying a beginner's book on trigonometry and teaching it to myself. In my own way, I corrected my past misdeed.

So many times I have heard the phrase, "God'll get you for that," and I never realized that it was not God, but myself that would track me down and correct the error. To paraphrase *A Course in Miracles*, "Errors only call for correction, never punishment."

Life is gentle. Your lessons are gentle. Surrender to them and learn. This is how we stretch and grow. And in the process we develop a lifelong romance with ourselves.

# Self Discovery Quiz

- *Do you constantly find yourself being attracted to toxic relationships (abusive, alcoholic, etc.)? Why do you feel that you insist on these experiences? What are your beliefs about yourself and love?*

- *Do you keep creating the same job, over and over? Have you ever asked yourself where you got the thoughts that jobs should not be enjoyable? Do you have a secret dream that you are afraid to take action on? If so, when will you do it?*

- *If you find yourself in unhealthy patterns, what is it that attracts you? What are the feelings or actions that are positive? For example: Maybe you are attracted to angry people because they have a lot of passion and energy. How can you create this passion and energy without the anger and attack?*

- *If you had a son or daughter who was living your life, what advice would you give them? Would you judge them?*

- *Do you stay stuck in a particular pattern because it absolves you from any actual growth or responsibility?*

- *Do you really believe that you can be a victim of circumstances?*

- *If Jesus found Himself making a mistake, what would He do?*

- *If Jesus found Himself in a toxic relationship or with toxic people, what would He do?*

*Once there was a student who wanted to be the best yogi in the world. And so he went away and practiced in a cave. Alone.*

*He practiced daily for twenty years. He studied, prayed, meditated and chanted. And after that time he could perform miracles.*

*He could walk on water. He could levitate. He could even manifest food out of thin air. He was indeed a powerful yogi.*

*One day he was in the marketplace of a nearby village with his Teacher and some other students. In the bustle of the crowd, somebody accidentally stepped on his foot. The student got angry and cursed the clumsy man.*

*His Teacher sadly looked at him and said, "It would have been better if you had spent the last twenty years in the marketplace."*

**Anonymous**

*Love is the greatest educational institution on earth.*

**Channing Pollock**

*I wish people who have trouble communicating would just shut up.*

**Tom Lehrer**

## Law #5:
# *"I Always Attract People Who Present Unlimited Opportunities for Learning"*

The *Teacher's Manual* of *A Course in Miracles* explains that long term relationships offer us *"unlimited opportunities for learning."* Many of our greatest "teachers" may be people we actively dislike. But the very things they do to upset us can open us up—if we are willing. There will be many times when we will feel misunderstood, judged or persecuted. Our choice then is to judge in return, or give ourselves the opportunity to see the situation with new eyes. We have unlimited opportunities to change our perception, to create a miracle. We have unlimited opportunities to forgive, or, if we prefer, to hold onto the hurt and pain.

If somebody approached me and said, "Boy, Jerry, that blond hair of yours really looks lousy today," it wouldn't bother me, other than thinking the other person is color blind. I have brown hair (albeit, *thinning* brown hair). I *know* my hair is brown. But let someone remark, "You are a great *Course in Miracles* teacher, Jer, but you know, you could drop a few pounds," and watch my defenses rise. They've touched on something about myself that I judge, for which I feel unlovable. Unless I realize this is the situation, I will believe that *those* people are hurting me. I will believe that they *made* me feel bad.

At this point, I have two options: I can get angry at them for "hurting" my feelings (which is what we've all done *ad nauseum*) or I can *use* my feelings to realize how insecure *I* am around this issue, and begin to take measures to correct it. Whether I lose weight or not is not the issue. The real issue is, "How do I feel about myself (or my weight) day to day, moment by moment?" When I take responsibility for my feelings and work on them, I become more grounded, easier to be around, and a more loving and lovable person. I may or may not choose to lose weight, but trying to blame the other person for my low self-esteem is just a repeat of all the old, blaming patterns from the past. It gets me nowhere and, ultimately, the friendship or relationship breaks up or becomes horribly suppressed.

We need to recognize that the world is always reflecting back to us our own thoughts. In short, the world is an accurate mirror of our inner thoughts and feelings. That is why we always attract people who tend to push our buttons. What we think is *out there* is actually already *in our minds*. Tell yourself the truth. Have you ever noticed that the people who have upset you in your life, really didn't tell you anything that you didn't already know and were afraid to admit to yourself? You already know you're fat, or bald, or insecure. You already feel bad enough about it. If you do not come to terms with whatever you are judging yourself for, if you allow it to subconsciously fester, you will then attract people *out there* to bring attention to these facts. Not because they are mean or like to pick on you, but because you are psychically shouting out to the universe, "Please help me come to peace with this issue (or my body, my thoughts, my job, or my money - whatever)!"

These people are like the little girl in the fairy tale of *The Emperor's New Clothes*. We want to strut and be adored while all the while we have issues we haven't addressed. And then we get mad at the little girl for telling the truth, that we are indeed not wearing any clothes.

Have you ever noticed that when something is bothering you, you constantly find your attention drawn to it? You know the feeling you have when there is a missing filling or a cavity in a tooth? Notice how your tongue plays with it, probes it, tests it. So, too, it is with our minds. We can try to deny that we have a problem, but our spiritual tongue plays and tests that emotional cavity. We can cover the hurt and low self esteem with jewels, fancy watches, new cars and high paying jobs that may give us a brief sense of relief. But ultimately, the true feelings emerge and those old buttons get pushed, one way or another.

Now, this does not mean that we should stay in relationships that are abusive and tell ourselves that this is for our highest good. The lesson we may need to learn is that we should not put up with any abuse and that we need to set limits. Standing on our own two feet and claiming that we will no longer tolerate abusive behavior is the most loving thing we can do for ourselves. It is also one of the best lessons we can learn. We can learn that we all have a right to be loved and respected—no matter what we have done in the past, no matter how much we earn, no matter whether we are skinny or overweight, black or white, gay or straight.

What it does mean is that rather than seeing ourselves as the other person's victim, we can take responsibility for our own unpleasant truths. It means being willing to see a part of us that still needs to be loved and accepted by ourselves. So instead of judging and defending against those "jerks" who point out your weight problem, you can take a deep breath, acknowledge the problem and then *decide* whether you want to do anything about it. Just remember, though, that as long as you *truly feel* that the weight is a problem, you will continue to attract people who will point it out.

One time, when I was a manager of a computer programming department, I was in charge of a new type of mortgage programming that we were developing for our clients' banks. Due to changes and enhancements that the users wanted, and also to modifications that made the system better, the project was late. Needless to say, my customers were upset and angry, and I worried about a meeting I was to lead concerning the delays. I was not looking forward to facing fifteen presidents and vice-presidents of these banks, and neither was my boss. In fact, at the last minute, he diplomatically backed out of the meeting, telling me he had the greatest confidence that I would do well. I felt abandoned, defensive and scared.

About a half-hour before the meeting, my girlfriend came up to me to give me some support. The night before she had attended a Unity church service and heard Alan Cohen speak.

"You know," she said, "Alan told us last night that your enemies can actually be your best teachers because they will tell you the unvarnished truth—whether you like it or not. In their own way they are loving you."

And she stuck a Post-It note onto my business notes, in which she had colored a picture of a rainbow.

"Just remember you are safe," she said. "Trust in love."

Whenever I hear a new thought that challenges and intrigues me, I like to play with it, and so, as I was walking toward the meeting, I began to play with my attitude about the meeting.

"What if," I said to myself, "these people are actually loving me in some weird way. What if they actually want me to succeed so much that they will do anything, including telling me the unvarnished truth, in order for me to get better? What if they are really interested in making a lot of money and *they want me* to make a lot of money too?"

And suddenly my attitude changed. Instead of these men and women being my adversaries, they were my friends! They were going to make me succeed whether I liked it or not!

I took a deep breath, said a quick prayer, and walked into the room feeling defenseless, safe *and* still a little apprehensive. Instead of trying to protect myself, I started the meeting with the announcement that the project would take another two weeks before completion. Then I took a breath and calmly passed out handouts of all the new enhancements and reports and began explaining why the project implementation had been pushed back. The new system was actually better and more versatile than the originally proposed system, and it was taking me longer to test all of the changes.

The managers looked at the proposed reports. Several of them commented on how much easier their jobs would be with the new enhancements. A few even had suggestions that would enhance the system even more. To my surprise, everyone seemed to have forgotten about the delay. One president even remarked that it was worth waiting an extra two weeks for the new changes we were implementing.

At one point, though, a manager began complaining loudly that we hadn't kept our word and that the project was still late. Before I could respond, two other people told him to pipe down and to look at the enhancements I was proposing. I left that meeting feeling that I had gained fifteen new friends and that the animosity which had been growing, was gone. Two weeks later, right on schedule, the new system went live. Our computer firm was the first company in the country to implement this new kind of loan, and in fact, for years afterward, we had other companies buy the system we developed for their uses.

Those wonderful managers presented me with a perfect opportunity to grow. I learned that instead of attack and defense, being honest and defenseless was a better way. I learned that bank presidents were not what I thought they were. I also learned that it was a little safer to be in this world and to trust in a loving God.

One of the most gentle and smart teachers I ever knew was my grandfather. He had a quiet, knowing way of teaching. He never made you feel stupid even as you learned. He also let you make your own mistakes without making you feel wrong.

One time my father wanted to install three windows in our house. John, my grandfather (my mother's father), was, among other trades, a carpenter, and so my dad asked him to help him install the windows. John came over and proceeded to show my father how to do the job, gradually letting him do more and more of the work. When the first window was finished, my grandfather said that he had to go home for supper, and left for the day.

The next day my father waited for John to show up. He didn't. Mom asked my dad why he didn't proceed with the windows.

"I'm waiting for John to come back."

"He's not coming back," replied my mom with a smile.

After a few days, my father gave up waiting and completed the job himself. As he was finishing the last window, my grandfather miraculously returned. He inspected the work my father did, checking the window operation to see how smoothly they opened and closed. He nodded in approval as each window passed inspection.

"Good job," he said. My dad felt proud that he learned a new skill and a greater love for his father-in-law, who first taught him and then allowed him to finish alone.

A well-known saying goes, "When the student is ready, the teacher will appear." How many teachers have appeared in our lives and we never recognized them? How many people did we have relationships with, people who aggravated us, people who hurt us, people who loved us and people who pushed us? When we begin to look at all the people who had an effect on our lives, we can actually begin to thank them for our lessons. Because as we learn from each person and correct our errors one at a time, ultimately we will become the person we've always wanted to be.

When I took my Six Month Program (an intense class in personal responsibility and ego-busting), I had fifteen female classmates who were committed to telling me their truth about me. I didn't like it. It was more comfortable to stay the same and live in my illusions that I was a "nice" guy. Instead, they confronted me with my games, my manipulations, my sexist thoughts, my attack thoughts and my secret judgments.

Slowly, I began to realize why my past relationships broke up. I was able to see the female side of my issues. Rather than judging me and writing me off (which is what happened in the past), these women persisted in telling me their truth, while still seeing the Divine nature that was in me. They saw possibilities in me. They were *more committed to my growth* than to being "right" in believing that men were not able to change. The wonderful thing is that, as I changed, we all changed and grew together.

You will find that we all play a beautiful part in each other's lives. There is nobody who is extraneous. As my teacher used to say,

"There are no *extras* on the planet."

We are all enrolled in a wonderful class of Life and we each have our part to teach and learn.

# Affirmations

- *People who push my buttons are simply my Divine Self trying to get my attention.*
- *I now use the mirror instead of the magnifying glass when looking at problems in my life.*
- *I will never die from being shown a side of myself that I am ashamed of.*
- *God in me is bigger than any problem that I can cause.*
- *God in me rejoices when I face my errors and correct them.*
- *I am never upset for the reason I think.*
- *I now bless the many people who have done their part to heal me.*
- *Dear God, push my buttons gently, so that I may heal gently!*
- *Nobody has ever lost from my becoming a better person.*

# Foundations of a
# Conscious Relationship

*Jesus said that a house built on sand will be washed away in the first big storm. So too, many relationships are built on sand. When we base our relationship on a cute body, money, security or a "solid" career, we are building on sand. The following section contains basic foundations that will solidify and strengthen your relationship.*

*A caress is better than a career.*
**Elisabest Marbury**


*Love is the heart's immortal thirst to be*
*completely known and all forgiven.*
**Henry Van Dyke**


*Marriages are made in heaven —*
*so are thunder and lightning.*
**Clint Eastwood**


*My wife and I have an agreement*
*that we never go to sleep*
*when we are mad with each other.*
*It works!*
*I haven't slept in three days.*
**Morey Amsterdam**


*My father hates that I am a Buddhist,*
*but he loves when I am Buddha.*
**From a story in *A Path with Heart* by Jeck Kornfield**

# Get Connected

The major factor in 80% of divorces and breakups is not:

*Affairs . . .*

*Financial difficulties . . .*

*Too much fighting . . .* or

*Sexual desire differences.*

In our experience, the biggest cause of divorces is simply *a lack of connection.* What Stav and I hear a lot from couples who broke up is that "we just grew apart." People may be in a relationship for years and suddenly realize that they are not lovers or partners, they are roommates—two people sharing the same space, but having no intimate connection to each other. They may know the day-to-day activities of each other's lives, but beyond that there is nothing.

Affairs develop due to a loss of connection. When a partner no longer feels connected to his/her mate, the partner may look elsewhere. Fighting is **not** a predictor of a breakup because, believe it or not, fighting is at least connection at some level. When done responsibly, fighting can be very healthy because it releases any emotional traffic jams. But even if the fighting is done wrong, even if it's at an unhealthy level, at least *some communication* is occurring. If the couple can learn how to listen and share differences responsibly, this will actually increase the likelihood of the relationship lasting.

We actually have this crazy idea that if we can keep ourselves separate from someone, if we can hold onto our secrets and judgements, if we can withhold intimacy, we will have a sense of safety. Being separate is an easy way of maintaining the illusion of control. As long as you don't let a person in, he/she cannot upset and change your life.

Even in the best of cases, our egos will slowly shut down the connection and intimacy between two people—until they become aware of the situation and take steps to correct it. Like many couples, Stav and I live life in fast-forward. Between counseling private clients, programming computers, teaching classes, writing books and giving speeches, we find that there is little time left for us to relate, and we end up neglecting our one-on-one contact. Many evenings our relating involves seeing each other around 9:00 at night, sharing a snack while we share our day and trudging off to bed. Our sharing at this time tends to be shallow, usually involving how our day looked, but not a whole lot about feelings, our needs or any issues that need to be addressed.

Since change does not come easily, most of the time we just let things remain as they are. But over a period of time the cost of separateness and isolation begins to take its toll. We feel a *loss of connection*. We find that we aren't as loving to each other. We snap at each other for little reasons. We get crabby. She doesn't feel loved. I don't feel appreciated. We don't like each other. And the gap between us widens.

This is where the commitment in a relationship gets tested. The truth is, it's always easier to just let things be. It's easier for me to play on my computer, surf the Internet or even write this book ("Don't bother me now! Can't you see I'm writing a chapter on connecting?"), than to relate to my wife. There is this part of me that wants to be separate, to be alone—to just have my own little world, where I control everything and all is neat and tidy. But by doing this all the time I lose my connection with my wife. And there is a part of me that KNOWS that I am neglecting hurting our emotional bonding.

Believe me, I am good at disconnecting from my feelings. I am good at *thinking* everything is fine, when in actuality my relationship is faltering. But Stav is a lot more honest and she tends to be my emotional touchstone. When she feels that we are losing connection, she lets me know. What I usually do is deny, argue and accuse her of wanting too much from me—hardly the kind of tactics to use in deepening a relationship.

What I feel at times like this is that she is trying to take away MY time. I am in fear—fear of losing control, fear that she wants ALL of my time, fear that I'll never get to do the things I want to do (by the way, these happen to be very old childhood fears of mine). Invariably we get into a fight. How long we fight depends upon my willingness to see her side.

But you know what I have learned? My partner does not want ALL of my time. She just wants SOME of my time. She doesn't require 24 hours-a-day attention (which is what my ego tells me). But she does want to know that she is loved and appreciated. And, funny thing, I also want the same things. After I finally stop arguing and we start connecting, I always enjoy the reconnection. I always feel emotionally filled and loved. And the argument always feels stupid and pointless. The truth is, the hardest part in connecting is overcoming the initial inertia and our fear of being controlled. After that it's always easy!

What we find that helps us is to literally set aside time to relate. Our favorite way is to take a long bath together. We dim the lights, light some candles, pour some wine, play soft music and sink into the warm water. And we just sit and enjoy the feeling of the water caressing us. We let the world go. And we talk and touch. It never seems to fail to open us up and reconnect our spirits.

Another great way to quickly increase connection is simply to hold each other. I mention this several times in this book because Stav and I find it is the easiest and quickest way to connect. For extra credit, hold each other naked.

One of the easiest ways to get connected is to learn to play with each other. Plan time to have fun again. Playing is another way of connecting.

John Gray, the author of *Men are from Mars, Women are From Venus*, tells of the time that he realized how present and connected he is with his private clients, and yet, after a hard day, he was not present for his wife. He would "hide in his cave" and read the newspaper or watch TV in order to decompress at the end of the day. Not surprisingly this caused some problems.

And so he implemented a simple plan. He decided to make his wife his last client of the day. He stretched his workday out for an extra half-hour. And that last half-hour was to be spent connecting with his wife.

## Four Minutes to a Better Relationship

John Gottman, Ph.D. in Seattle, WA. was studying tapes of couples as they fought and attempted to resolve differences. He theorized that what happened in the first fifteen minutes of an argument would determine how the argument continued and whether or not the couple could reach an agreement. And indeed by watching facial expressions, body language, the tone of voice and how each partner presented their side, his theory showed that what happened in the first fifteen minutes determined the rest of the argument.

Then, in order to be able to save time and money, his team shortened the time to twelve minutes. They found that they could predict the same results in twelve minutes.

They then shortened the time to nine minutes. They could predict the same results.

Six minutes. They could predict the same results.

Three minutes. They could *still* predict the same results.

What they realized was that how the couple related in the first three minutes determined how the couple would relate at the fifteen-minute point and that would continue throughout the argument. *How they **started out** determined how they **ended***. If the couple started out shouting, blaming and accusatory, the issue was rarely resolved. If, however, there was a *soft startup* (non-accusatory, gentle, safe)—especially by the women—**and** a *willingness* for the man to **listen** and **surrender**, they found that there was a greater chance of the argument being resolved peaceably. Gottman also found this to be an accurate predictor of whether the couple would make it in the long run or whether they would end up in divorce.

This actually makes sense. Chaos Theory, a branch of scientific study teaches that a miniscule action *during a moment of change* can have massive effects. A common Chaos Theory quote is,

"A butterfly, flapping its wings in China, can cause a hurricane in the Atlantic."

Basically Chaos Theory says that when change occurs, the *moment of transition* holds the *greatest opportunity* for benefit or disaster. What occurs at the beginning cascades into effects much bigger than the original incident. For example, one tiny rock, rolling down a mountain, depending on the path is takes, can cause a landslide. One snide remark can wreck an evening. A kind word can stop an argument. Or a moment of true listening can prevent a divorce.

So how does this lead to Four Minutes to a Better Relationship? Pat Love, Ph.D. believes (and I wholly agree with her), that the crucial point in a relationship is when a change occurs—the moment of transition. And instead of three minutes, actually only one minute is needed. In most relationships, there are at least four of these crucial points each day. These crucial moments are:

- When we first awaken.
- When one of us leaves for work.
- When we return from work.
- When we go to sleep.

Connecting with your partner at these times determines how you will relate to each other later on. Even if you're not fully awake and even a little grumpy, sharing a hug and a caress for a moment will start your day on a better foot. When one of you leaves for work, a kiss and a hug sends you both off with better spirits. Coming home and just momentarily acknowledging each other reestablishes the connection. And briefly connecting before falling asleep leaves you with a sense of peace and security.

Another moment of transition to be aware of is, for example, when you are both at the shopping mall and you decide to go your separate ways for a few hours. Connect for a second before separating. That's all it takes!

There have been so many times that I have had arguments with my partner because I hadn't done a simple act of connection. All it takes is one minute four times a day to connect with your partner. Give yourself an investment guaranteed to reap huge rewards. All it takes is four minutes!

## Increasing Your Connection by Releasing

Not only is it important to develop connections, but is it also important to become aware of anything that interferes with that connection. One major factor that erodes the connection between two people is holding onto unresolved feelings from past relationships. It doesn't matter if these feelings are negative or positive; either way they still affect your current relationship because you are still *emotionally connected* to someone from your past. It may show up as yearnings of past love, feelings of guilt and regret, or gnawing unforgiveness.

Do you have articles of clothing, an old hairbrush, or a book from a past relationship that still have strong feelings attached to them? I'm not saying that you should not possess photos or other mementos, but if you are still *strongly attached* to certain items from a past relationship, just know that you have not completely released that person. *That person is still in your life.* And as long as you still have this attachment to this person, you cannot be totally present for your present relationship.

It does not mean that you cannot still feel love for somebody from your past. In fact, this is very healthy. But when we hold onto old reminders that are very special to us, or we find ourselves daydreaming about "what might have been" or "I wish I had. . ." we are still hanging onto him/her.

If this is going on, I suggest you perform a ritual of letting this person go. It does not have to be anything special or hard. It can be as simple as lighting a candle, meditating and praying over the person, and sending them love. You may say a phrase such as:

*I now totally release you, (___name___). I release you financially, emotionally, romantically, psychically, physically and spiritually. I release you to your own life. I owe you nothing and you no longer owe me anything. You are now free. I am now free. If there is any forgiveness still to be done regarding you, I now take total responsibility for doing it. You no longer have anything to do with my pain.*

Then gently blow out the candle as you release that past love. You may actually feel a sense of relief as you let go of this stuck energy. If you find that you still have an old book, clothes, record albums or anything else from a past relationship, be willing to release them. Return the articles to their rightful owner or give them away. If old photos or mementos are getting in the way, pack them up and store them in a safe place—out of sight. Over time, those feelings and attachments will dissipate as you now strengthen your feelings for your current partner. Also let your partner know what you are doing so that they can support you. You may even be an inspiration for them to let go of any old relationships in their past.

Bob Mandel, in his book, *Two Hearts Are Better Than One*, breaks down the word intimacy into "*into-me-see.*" The greatest fear we have is the fear of facing ourselves—the fear of getting with our self. You will discover, though, that there is nothi because there is nothing that cannot be corrected or forgiven. Opening to another person opens you to yourself and vice-versa.

Spending time connecting with your partner is the best investment in time that you can make. Many times in my life, a three-hour argument could have been avoided with only a few minutes of connection. The hardest part is always the beginning. It's hard getting out of our inertia and actually changing our behavior, but in reality the cost of this change is always miniscule compared to the cost of being separate. To paraphrase Ellen Kreidman from her book, *Light Her Fire*,

"Five minutes of connection equals five hours of harmony."

Open up to your partner. Open up to yourself. You'll never regret the connection.

# Affirmations

- *I am now willing to be more intimate with myself.*

- *I never lose when I open to another.*

- *Connecting with my partner always leads to more peace and love.*

- *Connecting with my partner feeds my soul.*

- *My fear of intimacy is my fear of myself. There is nothing to fear inside of me.*

- *There is nothing to fear inside my partner.*

- *I love giving love. It is safe to be strong and give support.*

- *I love receiving love. It is safe to be vulnerable and receive love.*

- *I am never too busy to open up to my partner.*

# Fifty Ways to Love Your Lover

Tell them *"I love you"* - **often**

**Have breakfast in bed**

Touch each other often

*Leave love notes in random places*

Surprise your partner with flowers

**Honor their feelings**

*Give a back rub*

**Brag about them to others**

Spend 5-10 minutes when you first come home relating to your partner **before** you do anything else

*Wash each other's hair*

*Buy him/her candy*

**Give acknowledgments**

Massage each other's feet

*Just hold your partner - without talking*

Don't offer advice – listen

*Take naps together*

*Be on time*   *Have their car washed*

*Write a love letter*   **Go on a picnic**

WRITE A POEM   Cook something special

**Surprise them with a stuffed animal**

*Call them at work and tell them you love them*

Be attentive to your partner when you are in public

*Take a walk in the park*

*Go to a romantic movie (or rent one)*

**Buy him/her a greeting card for no reason at all**

**Buy their favorite cologne (perfume)**

Give frequent hugs  ***Listen to romantic music***

Go to bed at the same time

*Take a bath together*    Surrender, surrender, surrender

Let them know that you appreciate what they do for you

*Spend time together—alone*    ***Go to the beach***

BEFORE GOING TO WORK ALWAYS GIVE THEM A KISS

**Get into bed naked and hold each other**

Go to an art museum

Go dancing or take lessons

*Fly a kite*  **Hold hands when walking**

*Read to him/her in bed*  *Go to a play*

**Touch each other for no reason at all**

GET DRESSED UP AND GO OUT ON THE TOWN

Help them when they are tired

Ask your partner how they want to be loved

Meet him/her for lunch

*If you don't find balance between pressure and pleasure, your epitaph is going to read, "Got everything done, died anyway."*

**Paul Pearsall**

*You can indeed afford to laugh... Remember that God goes with you wherever you go.*

***A Course in Miracles*** Workbook Lesson 41

*I was trying to daydream but my mind kept wandering.*

**Steven Wright**

*Maintaining a complicated life is a great way to avoid changing it.*

**Elaine St. James**

© Lynn Johnston Productions Inc./Dist. By United Feature Syndicate, Inc.

# Are We Having Fun Yet?

One of the fundamental cornerstones for a healthy relationship is having the ability to play, have fun and laugh together. In fact, the ability to laugh at ourselves has been shown to be a *major predictor* for a satisfying, stable marriage. Isn't that why we get into relationships in the first place—to share with another and to enjoy life? I think that too many times partners in relationships lose contact with that original purpose. We get worn down by life, by our jobs, by the daily grind. We worry about the economy, our children's education, the bills, our career. And we forget why we originally fell in love with this person.

So, do you enjoy being with your partner? Do they challenge you and laugh with you and help you to grow? Is there a sense of joy in your interactions? Do you take time to play and interact? If these qualities seem to be missing in your relationship, remind yourself of how you were and how he/she was when you first met. Remember the ease, the joy, the fun you had. And then remind yourself that those feelings are still available to be felt.

*A Course in Miracles* states, *"To heal is to make happy."*

**Text Pg. 66 / 72**

Reflection on this thought led me to think about how important enjoyment is in our relationships. That is what this book is intended to do—to help you to regain your happiness in relationship with yourself and others. After all, if you are not having fun with your partner, why are you with him/her?

Now, don't get me wrong. We **do** need to process our issues and handle our life challenges, but sometimes we take ourselves too seriously. We need to lighten up. We don't need to process all of our issues *all the time,* analyzing every little incident. We must give ourselves time to let it go and to just simply enjoy life. Often the answer to a perplexing problem will only become apparent as we let it go, as we relax.

Spend time together to play and relate. Spend a weekend where you do not talk about your jobs, the kids, financial issues or the house. All you do is talk about yourselves. Find out if you really *like* each other. It's not the end of the world if you find that you do not like each other because now you can do something about it. At least now you have identified a problem. You can talk, you can get into therapy, you can meet with a minister, you can take workshops. Be willing to take this chance to regain a sense of joy and love in your relationship.

Recently my wife, Stav, and I spent a whole month vacationing on the island of Cyprus (Stav's homeland). We had lots of time to do nothing—sit on the beach, take long walks to visit her mom, souvenir shop or just find a place to eat.

Normally I keep myself busy with working on my computer, playing video games or reading, but on this trip I had no computer and so for awhile I read a lot. It's my way of being in my own world. But as I finished my book, something inside me resisted getting another one. I started slowing down and began to just hang out with Stav. And we found that we genuinely like each other's company. We remembered why we fell in love with each other—the love we have for people, our love of God, how blessed we feel to have each other, and just how easy it is to talk.

We spent time enjoying the simple, little pleasures of life. Having a cappuccino, sharing ice cream, sitting in the sun, watching a movie. And we enjoyed the simple, little pleasures of each other. A simple, "I love you," a touch, a caress, a laugh.

When you allow a sense of play and laughter into your relationship, you automatically let in God. Because, in my opinion, God is the Father (and Mother) of play and laughter. He/She *is* love and joy. And in those times when we really think our problems are *so bad*, God steps in and lovingly helps.

One time, very early in our marriage, Stav and I were having a real knockdown, drag-out fight. We were furious with each other! We were angry! We were actually screaming in each other's face, raging like maniacs. We were not about to let the other person win!

I was in the midst of a tirade, ranting at her, when suddenly I stopped, cold. And glaring at her with clenched teeth, I said,

"And do you know what else I'm really angry about?"

"No! What!" she yelled.

"I'm mad that *I forgot* what I'm mad about!"

She glared back at me and replied, "ME TOO!"

"Well I'm still mad at you," I countered.

"So am I."

We stared at each other for a moment longer, trying to stay mad, but finally we both exploded into laughter. We couldn't help it! We were still mad at each other, but we couldn't remember why. The laughter softened the moment.

Later we remembered why we were so angry, but you know what? It no longer mattered. It was no longer an issue. What seemed so irreconcilable earlier, now was nothing.

I recall another time, many years before, when I was driving home with my girlfriend from a family function. We were having a heated argument, and I was hot and righteous. I yelled and gesticulated as I drove through the rain-soaked Chicago streets. And just as I was really heating up, a car, coming from the opposite direction, hit a deep puddle of rainwater, sending a tsunami through my open car window. I continued driving, trying to keep my anger and composure, trying to act as if nothing had happened, while my girlfriend's body jerked in spasms as she tried not to explode in laughter.

I looked at her, water dripping off my nose and said,

"Well, I guess God's trying to tell me to cool off."

I did.

Another way of lightening up is to give yourself something that you secretly desire. Many times we deny ourselves simple pleasures and joys because we judge them as being silly. We deny asking our partner for a simple pleasure because we think they'll think we are immature or needy. We even deny giving ourselves the little things we desire, thinking we have to live up to some unspoken standard. We don't share our little upsets with our partner because we judge our upsets as silly and little. And yet, it is the little things, the simple pleasures, that build the lives we share.

One night after a very hard class day, I decided to rent a movie. I stood in the store looking at all the movies, trying to decide what I wanted to watch.

"Get something *good*," said my mind. "Get something socially significant. Get an Oscar winner like *Schindler's List* or *Terms of Endearment*."

As I was scanning the movie rack I suddenly spotted the movie *Wizards* – an animated cartoon. It tells the story of a post nuclear war world in which wizards, fairies and magic return and the ensuing conflict between magic and technology. I had heard about the movie years before and had always wanted to see it.

But then my mind kicked in again.

"Don't get a *stupid* cartoon! What good is that? Get a *good* movie that will teach you, one that will make you better and help you grow!"

I stood there for awhile, undecided, torn between what I *wanted* and what I thought was *good*. Finally I went inside and asked my child what I *really* wanted to watch. And the little child said, "*Wizards*." I rented the movie and I loved it!

I realized later that for the state of mind that I was in that night, the movie was exactly what I needed. I had spent a whole day processing people and working on problems and I needed something fun and mindless, something with no socially redeeming value other than it was fun.

Open up to the joy and fun that is possible in your life. There are thousands of ways to enjoy yourself and another. *To heal is to make happy*. As you take life less seriously, as you find humor in life's absurdities, you can nurture the playful child in you and help your partner do the same. Rest assured that your relationship with yourself and your partner is now on solid ground.

---

## Self Discovery Quiz

- *Is there something that you want that you deny yourself? When will you give it to yourself?*

- *Do you feel guilty or judge yourself or your partner when you are not doing anything constructive?*

- *Do you keep yourself from playing until all the chores are done?*

- *Would you like a foot massage, a back rub or just a cuddling session with your partner? When will you ask for one?*

- *What simple, little pleasures do you judge as silly or immature? Even though they may be silly and immature, do you want them anyway?*

- *Have you ever been in a bad mood and people or situations arise that can change that mood, but you hang onto the bad feelings? Why?*

- *When you were growing up, were you allowed to play?*

- *When you were growing up and you received money, how did you spend it? Did you enjoy it, hoard it, spend it all?*

- *Is there a movie that you have secretly wanted to watch, but were afraid what others may think?*

*While you are waiting for your ship to come in,
it helps to do some work on the dock.*

**Anonymous**


*An appeaser is one who feeds a crocodile
- hoping it will eat him last.*

**Winston Churchill**


*People have got to think.
Thinking isn't to agree or disagree.
That's voting.*

**Robert Frost**


*Appeasers believe that if you keep
throwing steaks to a tiger,
the tiger will become a vegetarian.*

**Heywood Broun**


*Namaste - The Divinity in me
honors the Divinity in you.*

**An Indian Greeting**

# Develop Healthy Boundaries

Whenever you see a relationship in trouble, you can count on the fact that neither partner has a healthy set of boundaries. Without boundaries, individuals do not know what limits to set on themselves and, more importantly, on others. As children, many of us experienced that our boundaries were not respected. For example, our parents may have come into our rooms whether we liked it or not, or our belongings were not respected and, in many cases, our feelings may not have been respected. And if nobody taught us how to set healthy boundaries, we then erected barriers in self-defense.

A barrier is an invisible wall, an imaginary locked door, a defense used to keep others *out* and ourselves protected. The very walls that protect us, however, keep us lonely and isolated.

Judgments and defenses are examples of barriers that we create. Some examples are: "Men are the problem and I'll never let them in," or "Women cannot be trusted. I tried once but I got hurt. Never again," or "Black people can't be trusted," or "White people only want to use people," or "That religion is the wrong religion and they are all going to hell!" These are all psychological barriers that we have erected to defend ourselves from some hurt we experienced in the past, or to deny our own low self-esteem. We may have totally suppressed the hurt and forgotten the incident that caused the original pain, but the barriers remain, and anytime we feel threatened, we automatically put up the defenses. Barriers are meant to keep pain out. Unfortunately, not only do they **not** keep pain out, but they also keep people out.

Boundaries, on the other hand, allow people in—*with permission*—as long as we are respected. In developing a healthy sense of boundaries, we need to dismantle the barriers and learn to define our *personal* space. Boundaries are invisible "fences" that serve three functions:

- To keep people from invading our personal space and abusing us, mentally, physically, emotionally, psychologically or spiritually.

- To keep us from invading other people's space and abusing them.

- To give us a sense of who we are.

For example, a personal boundary can be likened to the boundary that exists between Texas and Louisiana. It is not a physical boundary. You cannot see it. When you leave one state and enter the other, there is no indication that you have entered another state (other than a possible road sign). However, once you are in Louisiana, there are different laws in effect, and you better know what they are. If you ignore these laws and do not respect them, you will be fined.

The same exists for our inner boundaries. We need to develop the laws that we expect others to honor when they are in our space. It's about honoring yourself and honoring another. We need to develop inner laws such as:

"Name calling is not allowed when we're fighting."

"You are not allowed to hit me."

"You are not allowed to take my things without asking my permission."

"You do not make decisions that affect me without consulting with me first."

"I do not have sex on the first date and I expect that rule to be respected."

There is a saying, "We always teach others how we want to be treated." When we allow someone to abuse us, emotionally, physically or spiritually, what are we teaching the other person? That it is OK to hurt us—that we will not do anything about it. Relationships give us many opportunities to set our boundaries. They push us to define who we think we are, what we expect from ourselves and others, and how we want to be treated. And then relationships prompt us to *let others know* that it is not all right to defile our spirit, invalidate our emotions or crush our dreams.

Developing healthy boundaries is crucial because, when we know our limits and needs, then we can communicate them to others. When we tell others our expectations, they then get to decide whether they want to go along with us or not. The wonderful part is, as we develop and express ourselves, others will follow our example and also grow and express themselves. Too many times I see people who stay in abusive relationships because they made a vow of "until death do us part," or they think that it is *spiritual* to suffer and that is what God wants. What God wants us to do is to be happy and set limits on any behavior that hurts us.

Setting healthy boundaries helps us to see the Christ in another without having to put up with abusive behavior. I had a client who had a hard time being willing to see the Christ in her ex-husband because of the abuse she had sustained. She once told me, "If I am willing to see the Christ in him, if I am willing to see the good in him, that means I will *have* to go back to him. And I don't want to go back to him!"

So I asked her, "Do you believe that God is everywhere?"

"Yes, I do," she replied.

"So the spirit of God is in that chair that you're sitting on?"

"Yes."

"And God is in me?"

"Yes."

"And God is in you?"

"That one I have a hard time with, but I'm willing to see that."

"OK. So you really *do* believe that God is in everything."

"Yes."

"Is the spirit of God in a rattlesnake?"

"Yes," she answered slowly.

"Well if God is in rattlesnakes, why don't you play with them?"

"Because they're dangerous, they'll bite me."

"Exactly. It is the rattlesnake's nature to attack and defend itself, so much so that it is dangerous. The same is true for your ex-husband. Even though the spirit of God is within him, right now, his nature is too dangerous for you to be around at the present time. Right now, the most loving thing you can do is to take care of yourself and stay away."

She felt relieved to know that she could set her own boundaries and that being willing to see the Christ in her ex-husband did not mean that she had to be with him or condone his actions.

Setting up and communicating rules for how we want to be treated is not limiting, but freeing. If somebody wants to play football with us but doesn't want to follow the rules, we don't have to make them wrong. We can just say,

"Look, these are the rules that I play by. If you want to play with me, fine. I'd love to play with you. But if you don't want to honor my rules, then you'll have to play somewhere else."

Although my mother and father are in their sixties, they are still learning and growing. My mom and dad have worked together in their upholstery business for more than 40 years. He solicits the business and reupholsters the couches; she sews the patterns for the new couch. (You could say that even my parents are in recovery.) For many years, my mother put up with my father whenever he would get angry. He wasn't physically abusive, but he could get verbally derisive. Periodically, she would stand up for herself, but only when they were alone, because she didn't want to make waves in front of us kids or anybody else. She thought that that was what a *good wife* was supposed to do. For a time he would change, but slowly he would drift back to his old behavior. That is — until one day. . . .

She had sewn a piece of fabric for a couch and she had accidentally sewn it one inch too far. My father exploded. He ranted and fumed and called her a stupid idiot. That was it!

Without a word, my mother walked out into the courtyard, where the other businesses were located. Holding up the offending material for all to see, she began to shout,

"I'm such an idiot! Look everybody, I made a mistake. I'm so stupid! My husband is a saint for having to put up with someone as stupid as me!"

My father, on the side, was furiously whispering to her,

"Jean! What are you doing! Get back here and stop making a fool of yourself!"

But mom continued,

"And I'm a fool too. Oh, I'm **such** a fool! I don't know why my wonderful husband puts up with me! Look, I'm an inch off. I should have known better! I am so stupid!"

After a few more moments of this, my mother returned to the shop, putting the material back in my dad's hands. She looked him square in the eye and said,

"You wouldn't treat a hired person like you treat me! I am not stupid. And I am not a fool. Don't you ever call me that again! I make mistakes—just like you. I am **not** your idiot child and don't you ever treat me like one. If you do," and she pointed out to the courtyard, "I'll let everyone know again."

You know what? My dad has changed his attitude toward mom's occasional mistakes **a lot**. And on those rare occasions when he begins to lose his temper, she just looks him in the eye with that certain look and he remembers.

In that moment my mother created a boundary and claimed her identity. She still loves my dad. They still fight and argue, but name-calling is no longer allowed.

Setting a boundary will also take us into new territory and show us sides of ourselves that we didn't realize existed. When I was a teenager I was terrified of getting into fights. Not only was I not coordinated and strong, but also I had a secret fear that if anyone ever punched me in the face—it would explode. And so I never showed anger. This, of course, led to me sometimes being picked on.

In senior year, in gym class, we were playing touch football and of all people, I somehow ended up trying to block Dave Brickman — the class bully. He had this perpetual, arrogant sneer whenever he looked at me or any of my friends and he liked to push people around.

So, here I was, trying to block this guy and every time he pushed past me he clipped me on the chin with his elbow. I'd feel a flash of anger, but my fear was greater than my anger. And so I'd rub my chin and suppress my anger. Again we lined up. The ball was snapped and again I got clipped.

I don't know how many times he clipped me, but finally something broke. The last time, as he was rushing me, instead of blocking, I just hauled off and punched him square in the face!

Realizing what I had done, terror took hold, and I sped off across the football field with him in hot pursuit. I can still remember the coach screaming at us,

"Get back here, you idiots! I'm gonna kill you both! Get back here!"

But we ran and ran and ran until finally I could run no longer and panting, I turned around and faced Dave. We squared off and he punched me right in the face.

You know, to this day I do not remember any pain associated with that punch. I remember taking it and still remained standing as we glared at each other. We both stood there, panting and dead tired, the coach screaming at us, the class watching us and then Dave kind of nodded to me and began to walk back.

Nothing was ever said about the incident. It didn't change our feelings toward each other, but he and his pals never picked on me again. And when we played football, he stopped clipping me.

In utter rage, I had set a boundary and I had found out that I would not die if I was hit.

Now I want you to know that I do not approve of setting boundaries through violent methods. But I have found that sometimes, we may have to take drastic action in order to change the situation. What I feel happened to me is that my fear of standing up for myself and feeling my anger led to a feedback cycle that attracted more anger. In the end, I exploded because there was nowhere else to go.

I really don't know if there was any other way I could have handled that situation (I don't think Dave would have been open to a dialogue or mirroring process), but the earlier we can set our boundaries, the less likely we'll have incidents that lead to explosive ends.

Equally important is to set boundaries **around** your relationship. This helps a couple to develop an identity separate and apart from our extended families, old friendships, and even our children. Oftentimes we allow everybody and everything to impinge on us to the detriment of the relationship. Too many times we hear stories of children, in-laws, ex-spouses and friends causing havoc with a relationship. Spending too much time with an old buddy at the neglect of the partner indicates a poor relationship boundary. Similarly, maintaining contact with a previous lover (beyond normal arrangements when children are involved) or letting in-laws disrupt our lives is another example.

It is necessary that the partners agree *as a unit* what is and is not important. This is especially true if you have children. When the parents, as a unit, agree on what is and is not allowed, then the children cannot play one parent off against the other.

First checking with your partner before making commitments is another example of setting healthy boundaries around your relationship.

Setting boundaries is a high level of self-love. It is also a high level of love in a relationship. As you learn to honor and cherish yourself, you teach others to honor and cherish you. You are also teaching them to honor and cherish themselves. Barriers are designed to keep pain out, but unfortunately they also keep people out, they keep new ideas out and they keep love out. They also keep our pain in. Dismantle your barriers and draw new, solid boundaries. Choose the life you want. And then teach others to honor it too.

# Self Discovery Quiz

- *Do you know how you want to be treated by another person? Have you ever sat and written down how you want to be treated?*

- *Have you ever violated someone else's boundaries? How did it feel?*

- *Have you ever allowed somebody to violate your boundaries? How did it feel?*

- *Have you ever allowed somebody to convince you to do something that was unethical, immoral, or something you personally did not want to do? Will you allow it to happen again?*

- *Is it possible to set up boundaries without being abusive or controlling?*

- *When you actually tell a child or your partner exactly what you expect and want, do you think it makes it easier or harder for them to listen?*

- *What are your payoffs for being controlled and manipulated? Does it allow you to shift responsibility?*

- *What boundaries would Jesus suggest you might need to establish in your relationships? How would He go about setting them?*

*Pride goeth before the fall.*

**Proverbs 16:18**

*Embarrassment is the path back to God.*

**Rev. Phil Smedstad**

*Man is the only animal that blushes,
and has any need to.*

**Mark Twain**

*If fifty million people say a foolish thing,
it is still a foolish thing.*

**Anatole France**

*He missed an invaluable opportunity
to hold his tongue.*

**Andrew Lang**

"WHY DON'T WE JUST KISS AND MAKE UP
AND SAVE THE MONEY?"

© 1999 Reprinted courtesy of Bunny Hoest and King Features

# Let Go of Your Pride and Eat Some Humble Pie

Being in a relationship is a very humbling experience. In fact, *any* growth we make is a humbling experience for the simple reason that we are in new territory. In any learning situation, we should not be surprised by mistakes. In fact, we should expect them and be ready to forgive ourselves. This is a natural part of the learning process.

When we are taking new steps, we will be exposed to things about ourselves that we judge, aspects of ourselves that we would prefer that other people (us included) never saw. But, by seeing these aspects, we have the opportunity to do something about them. The choices are to either suppress them again or expose them— look at them, feel them and then do something different.

We like to see ourselves as *enlightened* and *loving*. It is embarrassing when we see something else in ourselves. In my classes, I usually have a brief exercise in which the participants mingle and tell each other an affirmation such as "God Himself is incomplete without me," "I now claim my magnificence," or "I am becoming perfect moment by moment." What comes up a lot is embarrassment, but, also, a lot of joy. At first, the people are scared to claim such a thought, but as they do, their bodies relax and they begin to laugh as they say it.

Many of us have been raised to believe that we are sinners, the misbegotten children of an angry God. We have been taught that we are nothing and that it is actually noble to feel unworthy. Many of us actually develop a sense of pride around our unworthiness. I find the hardest clients to work with are the ones who hang onto their guilt and feelings of unworthiness as if their guilt and unworthiness were precious jewels, unwilling to acknowledge that *maybe* they are deserving of love. This false pride keeps us holding onto thoughts that we are unworthy because we *think* we know who we are instead of *knowing* who we are. *A Course in Miracle* says,

> "To believe in your littleness is arrogant, because it means that you believe that your evaluation of yourself is truer than God's"

**Text pg. 166 / 179**

When somebody compliments you, do you ever feel a quick flash of embarrassment? Do you ever try to give the compliment back or make light of it ("This old thing? I got it on sale")? My friend, Rev. Phil Smedstad says, "Embarrassment is the feeling we get when other people are loving us more than we are loving ourselves." Being in relationship with another can bring up embarrassment from the feelings that arise when another person is simply loving and accepting us. The love is exposing more of our stuff that needs to be healed. *A Course in Miracle* states that it is love, not fear, of which we are truly afraid.

One way of letting go of your pride is to tell your partner you love him/her. Early in my relationship with Stav, she mentioned to me how she loved receiving roses. We didn't have a lot of money at the time, but one afternoon I happened to be passing a florist shop and they had roses on sale. So I bought three for Stav. The florist wrapped them up in green paper with a few stems of baby's breath, and I went home feeling excited. When I arrived, I saw that she was meeting with three of her friends. She saw the flowers in my hand and her eyes lit up.

"For me?" she asked.

Do you know those times when you do something *really* stupid and immediately wish you had stapled your mouth shut? This was one of those times. Having her friends there embarrassed me.

"Uh, no," I replied lamely. "They're for the house."

It didn't matter how many relationship classes I took. It didn't matter that I **taught** people how to have better relationships. Right in that moment I threw everything out the window. My strutting, macho male side could not acknowledge in front of a few women that I loved my wife! Later that day, I sheepishly admitted to her that I really did love her and that the flowers were for her not the house.

How many times do we neglect letting our partners know we love them because it may make us look weak? And yet, that is the very thing that strengthens a relationship. Letting the world know how much you love your partner is a powerful affirmation. Your partner feels loved and affirmed by you. One of the most common complaints in the couples that Stav and I see is that a partner does not show affection or interest for the other in public. Letting go of our pride gives us many opportunities to see how nutty and crazy we can be. But it also offers opportunities to become sane. Letting go of my pride and acknowledging my *little* thoughts, my *little* feelings, my *little* self is an important step in recognizing my part in the difficulties in my relationships and, thereby, opening up to my Divine self.

One night, after a terrible, frustrating day, I settled down to watch a video that I had rented. About a half-hour into the movie, Stav came home and wanted to relate. I wanted to watch my movie. After a few minutes of trying to get me to open up, she began to feel angry and hurt. I told her I didn't want to relate; I had just gotten interested in the movie and I didn't want to stop. She accused me of being autistic and separate (which was true) and stomped off saying that, since I didn't love her, **she** would love herself by going to the mall.

She left me watching my movie alone. By this time, I was seething. I couldn't enjoy the movie—she had ruined it for me. In a fit of childishness I ran into the garage and closed the garage door before she could back out.

"You're not leaving!" I yelled at her. "We are going to sit and relate!"

"You're crazy," she replied.

"You're damn right I'm crazy. But if you're going to spoil my evening, I'm going to spoil yours! So get out of the car and let's relate!"

She gave me that look she has when she knows I am totally in my ego, got out of the car and we returned to the living room—to relate. Of course, I was angry and stared stonily at the wall.

"Well?" she asked. "What do you want to say?"

"Nothing!" I said sullenly.

"If you're not going to talk, I'll just go to the mall."

"Oh no, you're not," I countered. "You've ruined my evening and so I'm going to ruin yours. You want **all** my attention. Well, now you've got it!"

Suddenly, she laughed at how stupid we were acting. I *almost* smiled, but quickly controlled myself and held onto my self-righteousness. She touched my hand.

"I just want a *little* of your time. I was not having a good day and I just want a little reassurance that you still care for me."

I blinked and felt my heart soften.

"You don't need to stop watching your movie," she said, "but let me in, too."

"Well, I had a rotten day, too," I said, as I finally allowed myself to acknowledge the feelings I was trying to avoid by watching the movie.

And we began to talk. We shared our feelings. I shared the hard day I had just experienced and how I just wanted to shut the world out. I just wanted to hide in my own little shell and protect myself. She shared her day and her frustrations and why she wanted some time with me. We both cried and laughed as we opened up to each other. It took all of fifteen minutes. Then, we held each other in love and in silence. After a few quiet minutes of holding, Stav looked up at me and said,

"So, can I go shopping now?"

We both burst out laughing.

"Yes. And can I go back to my movie?"

"Of course."

She went off to the mall and I restarted the movie where I left off. We both enjoyed ourselves apart, and later, when she got home, we enjoyed ourselves together.

What I learned from that experience was there are times when I have to let go of being an *adult* and let the brat out. It's not the end of the world. I realized that if I had just sat on those feelings, I would have ruined my evening and hers, and later we would have just gotten into another fight.

How many times do we hold onto our pride and not allow the little brat to be expressed? How many times do we want the other person to suffer? But since we are *above such actions*, we don't express that little brat; instead, we get even later around something unrelated to the original incident. How many times do we judge ourselves as being immature and then end up later acting immature anyway?

Releasing our pride is a lifelong occupation. It is upsetting to our egos but Divinely empowering. When my ego acts up and begins to strut and bluster, there are two things I usually do (once I get sane). First, I tell it, "Be still and know that I am God." Then, I imagine holding the little hand of a scared little four-year old boy (my ego is really just like a frightened child) and telling it,

"You are my creation. I will not destroy you. I will not hurt you. But, I will not listen to your rantings and ravings. I can change and will change. And you cannot stop me."

I find that when I relate to my inner brat (ego) with love and safety, it settles down. We only use pride because we are uncertain and afraid; we thought that our pride protected us. Instead it has given us the very things we tried to avoid: loneliness, low self-esteem, defensiveness, and pain. Don't be afraid to admit to your partner that you are wrong, or that you had a terrible day and you just want some loving. Don't be afraid to admit to those times when you feel needy. It takes more time and is more costly and painful to stay in our pride and push love away

Don't be too proud to take the time to love fully.

# Self Discovery Quiz

- *Which is more important, saving face or saving your relationship?*

- *What are you most afraid of asking for help in?*

- *Have you ever had a question but were too afraid to ask it because you were afraid of looking stupid? Did somebody else ask that same question and did you feel relieved? Did you judge that person for asking?*

- *Do you think that people who ask for help are dumb?*

- *Do you have love and compassion for a child who only wants to learn? Can you extend that same love and compassion toward yourself?*

- *Have you ever persisted in a fight, even after you realized you were wrong?*

- *Are you afraid to ask for help from your boss? Your coworkers? Your family? Your relationship? Your children?*

- *Have you ever asked a child for help or even advice? Have you ever asked a child to hold you when you felt down? Is a child's love worth less than an adult's?*

*No man is wise enough by himself.*
**Plautius**

*I use not only all the brains I have,*
*but all the brains I can borrow.*
**Woodrow Wilson**

*All men like to think they can do it alone,*
*but a real man knows there's no substitute*
*for support, encouragement or a pit crew.*
**Tim Allen, *Don't Stand Too Close to a Naked Man***

*I am not young enough to know everything.*
**J. M. Barrie**

*Life is like playing a violin in public*
*and learning the instrument as one goes on.*
**Samuel Butler**

# Ask For Help

It takes a lot of courage to ask for help, but when you do, the world will open up to you. Too many people think that they can solve their problems by themselves. They think that they don't need anybody's help. Some families do not want to "air their dirty laundry in public." Others believe that there is something wrong or shameful about asking another person for help. But this kind of thinking only keeps our problems from being solved.

We need to see that the world is full of people and experiences that can help us through any problem. There are many people in our lives who have experienced the same troubles we are having and have worked them out. There are trained therapists, counselors and ministers who can help you through the rough periods and help you to see that trust and love can support you in finding peace. Life is not a one-man band. It's a concert. We need to be willing to rely on other people's experience, to lead us, to teach us, to guide us back into sanity.

The most important lesson I feel I have learned in the last ten years is that **everybody** needs help at some time. Before then, I was too proud to ask for help. I was a loner, a survivor. I thought that asking for help was weak. It wasn't until I felt broken and despairing that I finally reached out for someone else to help me, to carry me for awhile, to guide me to sanity, and to teach me that I was still safe. Since that time, I have learned that the world is full of love, in more ways than I can imagine.

When asking for help, always select somebody who is expressing and living the life you admire. Going to the bar and complaining about your wife is the worst thing to do, unless you admire the people there. When I want support, I always ask some-body who I **know** will tell me the truth, whether I like what they tell me or not. I look for someone who isn't afraid that my love will go away if my feelings are hurt. I may not agree with what they say, but I will listen and check in with my heart to see what feels true. If I do not like hearing what they have said, I now know that there must be a kernel of truth in it. There must be some truth that I am not telling myself.

One of the greatest lessons we can teach our children is that we don't have to have all the answers. We just need to find the people who can help us to find those answers. One year I was tak-ing my daughter, Mary, out to buy some new clothes for her thirteenth birthday. She was at that gawky stage where her body was changing, and she was very shy about her figure. We went to the children's section to begin looking for outfits. Nothing fit. Af-ter about an hour of trying on all types of jeans and dresses, I could see that even though she was trying to hide it, Mary was definitely upset. We left the area and stood by the escalators.

"What do you want to do now?" I asked.

"I don't know! Nothing fits! I just want to go home!"

I took a breath and put my arm around her.

"You know," I said, "sometimes I really hate shopping for clothes because nothing seems to fit. Either they're too tight or they're the wrong color. It really puts me in a bad mood, too, when I can't find anything I like."

Mary began to cry a little, as I held her.

"So, are you willing to trust me, just for a little while?"

"Yeah."

"OK, here's what we'll do. First, let's go down to the Food Court, get us something to eat and a Coke. Then, we'll try the next three stores. We'll spend no more than an hour. If we **still** can't find anything, we'll go home and relax and let it go for today. OK?"

"OK," she smiled.

We took the next hour just hanging out, eating and letting the shopping experience dissipate. Then we were ready to try again. We went back to the same store, found a saleswoman and told her our problem.

"My daughter and I are trying to find clothes that fit her and nothing seems to fit. Can you help us?"

"Where were you looking?" she asked.

"In the children's section."

She sized Mary Jean up and replied, "She's a growing girl. You need to go to the Junior Miss section."

She proceeded to take us to the section and began selecting clothes that might fit. The selections were endless, and Mary Jean soon had five or six outfits to try on. And every outfit looked great!

But there was one outfit I *knew* she loved. Mary Jean came out of the fitting room wearing a blouse, tied across her midriff, and jean shorts, and she had a shy, hopeful, expectant look that every dad loves. You could tell by her face that she *loved* the outfit and *hoped* her daddy did too. I did.

"Wow! That looks great!"

She beamed at my acknowledgment. We selected the clothes she wanted and soon we were on our way. We both learned a lesson that day—to ask another person for help. God is in the world, in the form of many different people, just waiting for us to find Him. He has many unique answers to our problems. All we have to do is ask for some help.

# Affirmations

- *God in me is big enough to handle any lesson I need to take.*

- *I do not need to know all the answers. I only need to ask for help.*

- *I live in a world full of support. I now allow myself to ask for help.*

- *When I ask for help, the Universe rejoices.*

- *My life is not a one-man band. It is a concert.*

- *By asking for help, I give another person an opportunity to grow too.*

- *I am never healed alone.*

*When you talk you only say something*
*that you already know —*
*when you listen you learn*
*what someone else knows.*

**Anonymous**

*All man's miseries derive*
*from not being able*
*to sit quietly in a room alone.*

**Blaise Pascal**

*An apology is the superglue of life.*
*It can repair just about anything.*

**Lynn Johnson**

*Yearn to understand first*
*and to be understood second.*

**Beca Lewis Allen**

# Defenselessness – Dropping the Armor

To the world, the word "surrender" or the thought of being defenseless is anathema. We learn to expect the worst, to be prepared to fight for our rights, and that it is a jungle *out there*. If you are wedded to this state of mind, surrender, for you, would be stupid.

When we get into an argument, the *normal* method of arguing is that you accuse me of something, and then I defend my actions, and then I accuse you of something else, and you defend your actions. Attack - defend - attack - defend. Shoot - reload - shoot - reload. We argue about more and more different issues, all the while getting nothing resolved. And many times we end up arguing about something totally unrelated to the original topic.

When we are defensive, we are actually coming from a place of weakness because defensiveness means that we think there is *something* we need to defend *against*. We are trying to protect something (usually our pride or ego), against something else (the Truth).

What is a defense? My definition of a defense *is **any action** that **interrupts** a feeling or a truth from being felt and released*.

Some examples of defenses are:

- Being sarcastic or attacking when having an argument. Keeping the other person on the defensive.

- Not listening when your partner is sharing, but instead planning what you will say when you finally get your chance.

- Deflecting compliments – "Oh, this old thing? I bought it at K-Mart years ago."

- Changing the subject or joking when a sensitive subject is brought up.

- Buying things when you cannot afford them.

- Playing video games or surfing the Internet to excess.

- Saying, "I don't want to talk about it" when your partner brings up a sensitive topic.

- Using sickness or old unresolved grievances to keep others from handling your issues. "Oh, I can't talk about that right now. Your questions reminded me of the time my husband left five years ago, and my head just started hurting again."

- Lighting up a cigarette or grabbing a doughnut whenever you become upset.

- Working/exercising too much.

- Rolling your eyes or huffing when somebody brings up a grievance.

What do all of these actions have in common? Each of them is used to prevent the person from feeling an uncomfortable, underlying emotion. Attacking, accusing, or planning your strategy during an argument keeps your mind busy and defends you against possibly seeing the other person's side. Deflecting a compliment is a defense against possibly feeling your true feelings of unworthiness. Buying things you can't afford may keep you from feeling deprived and unworthy *for the moment*, but the resultant feelings of having to pay bills we can't meet revive those feelings once again. Keeping yourself busy with work, games, and the Internet distracts you from experiencing how you really feel about your life. Not talking about a painful topic keeps you from feeling bad *in the moment*, even though the suppressed pain will inevitably come out later.

So instead of letting the emotion come up, be acknowledged and released, the defense shoves the feeling *back down*, only to lie in wait for the next opportunity to be released.

Let me stress something here. I am not saying that playing video games, surfing the Internet, smoking, eating doughnuts, etc. are wrong or defenses in themselves. But when we use these actions to keep us from feeling an underlying emotion, that is when they become defenses.

As *A Course in Miracles* states,

*It is essential to realize that all defenses do what they would defend.*

**Text pg. 334 / 359**

The very things we do to keep those nasty feelings away actually aggravate the situation, priming us for the next time they will arise. Pushing away a compliment may keep us momentarily from feeling low self-esteem, but ultimately pushing away compliments make us feel unworthy anyway. Buying things when we cannot afford them may assuage a suppressed feeling, but later we are faced with the bill and the fear in trying to create the money to pay it off.

Take me, for example. The very things I did to defend myself caused the problems I thought I could run from. In an effort to be in control of my life, I became a very controlling man. If you ever want to guarantee being out of control, try being controlling. The more I tried to control my life, the more my life felt out of control. The more I tried to control my partner, the more resentful she felt, and the more she rebelled. It was a vicious circle that took some deep therapy for me to realize how *I* was causing the very problem I was trying to avoid.

When it came to a difference of opinion, I *always* had a reason for why I did what I did. I always had an excuse. I always had a handy defense. Once, in my Six-Month Program, somebody mentioned a character trait about me that I did not like.

"What do you mean by . . ." I started.

"You're defending yourself," said Joe, our teacher.

"But I just wanted to. . ."

"You're defending yourself," Joe repeated.

"But don't I get to…"

"You're defending yourself."

I shifted in my seat and pointed my finger.

"You're defending yourself, Jerry."

"But…"

"You're defending yourself."

I start to say something.

"You're *still* defending yourself."

I felt like a gasping fish left on shore. I'd open my mouth and Joe was there, reminding me that I was defending myself. I felt stuck. I felt that all I could do was listen and not say my side. And there was a part of me that was *convinced* that if I didn't get to say *my side*, then people wouldn't understand or like me. Actually, the real truth was that a part of me was afraid that I would be hated and ostracized. I didn't realize until later that Joe was trying to teach me that I didn't have to defend anything. As soon as I defended myself, I was weak. What I needed to learn was this: What feeling or truth was I trying to prevent myself from acknowledging?

Eight months later, during my Practitioner Training, I had an experience that really cemented the lesson. I was at the end of my rope. I felt that I couldn't go on. I was tired of trusting God, trusting my teachers and trusting my classmates. I felt I needed to stop surrendering and *get control of my life*. So, I decided to take a weekend retreat on nearby Whidbey Island (the Seattle area) to see what should be my next step.

I spent the weekend in silence, talking to nobody and taking long walks on the beach. One morning I was walking along the beach thinking about what I was going to say when I returned on Monday. I was having an inner argument with my teachers and classmates.

"I'll say this and then they'll probably say that, and then I'll reply with this argument, and then they'll probably say that and so I'll respond with this…"

On and on my mind went, spinning off strings of defenses and arguments to uphold my decision to quit and get a regular job.

Then suddenly, I got it! Joe, my teacher, was always telling me how defensive I was, how I couldn't hear anything because I was so busy planning my next word and counterattack. I realized that there I was—alone on that beach—with nobody for miles, and I was defending my position! I was fighting everybody in my class, and they weren't even there!

I realized how frail I thought I really was by the fact that I was always planning a defense, a rationalization for what I did, an excuse for any action I took. I couldn't just tell somebody my truth and then just let it be. I couldn't just tell my truth and face the consequences. No, I had to weave defenses around me, to protect what I imagined they would attack and disapprove of.

I laughed when I saw my insanity. And so I stopped thinking about how I would justify that I wanted to quit and get a job.

The following Monday I told Joe, "I've been trying to trust God all these months. I know He is there, but something is not working. Debts keep piling up, I have bills to pay and I cannot go on like this. I need a job. I need some stability."

"Do you want to quit the training?" asked Joe.

I thought for a moment and followed my heart. "No, not really, but I don't see any other way. I can't get a job **and** do the training, not with all the time it takes."

"Well, Jerry, if you could have it any way you wanted, what would you want?"

"To get a job at $20 an hour, work 20 hours a week and some-how continue my training."

And Joe turned to my classmates and asked, "Would you all be willing to let Jerry cut back on his duties here, so that he could get a job? Would you be willing to support him in what he wants, even though he won't be able to do all the jobs he was doing here?"

And you know what? My classmates supported me. They blessed me and told me to create that job and stay in the training. They *wanted me there*, with them, even though I couldn't be there all the time. I didn't need to defend myself or convince them. My sincerity, honesty and defenselessness convinced them. For once I was actually real. In that moment, I felt like I could cry for a thousand years. In all my years, I had never let other people's love in to that extent. I always kept a little part of me separate and right then I knew what I had been missing, what I had been defending myself from.

That week I polished up my resume and began applying for jobs. A week later I created a contract programming position at $20 an hour in which I could choose my hours. The final result was that not only was I able to create a job with the schedule and salary I wanted, but the aliveness and excitement I felt in having my life work gave me more than enough time and energy to complete my training. Not only did I not have to cut down on my training hours, but I had enough energy to be the editor of the newsletter.

I once read an Alcoholics Anonymous poem that illustrates how our defenses cause the very problems we are trying to run from.

## Why I Drank

*I drank to be witty - I became a bore*
*I drank to relax - I couldn't stop my hands from shaking*
*I drank to feel good - I had sickening headaches*
*I drank to be happy - it made me depressed*
*I drank to be a good dancer - it made me stagger*
*I drank to be a good conversationalist -*
　　　　*I couldn't even pronounce my name*
*I drank to be a good lover - I couldn't perform*
*I drank to be a man - I became a crying slobbering baby*
*I drank to be popular - I lost my friends*
*I drank for camaraderie - I drove everyone away*
*I drank to escape - I built a prison*
*I drank to find peace - and I found hell*

**Anonymous**

# *The Art of Defenseless Sharing*

When we have a disagreement, our defenses really get activated; it is then up to us to determine whether we will keep our defenses up or let them down. Have you ever noticed, when you're having an argument with your partner, that while he/she is speaking, you're thinking of your defense? You're planning a quick jab back, a smart remark, a way to attack and defend your position. And all the while an amazing thing is happening. **You're not listening!**

I remember seeing a cartoon of a couple sitting in a restaurant. And he's saying to his girlfriend,

"Why am I talking so loud? Because I'm wrong!"

So the next time you're having an argument or even a difference of opinion with a colleague—listen, listen, listen.

Listen - without thinking.

Listen - without analyzing.

Listen - without worrying whether what you **need** to say will get said. Put your defenses down for a moment and listen.

Listen and feel.

Don't think of yourself.

Don't think of a reply.

Don't think. Period.

Try to really *hear* what the other person is saying. Try to really understand how it *feels* to be that person and to see the problem through their eyes.

Don't be surprised if you find yourself fidgeting and squirming and wanting to jump up and leave the room. Don't be surprised if you find yourself extremely bored. That in itself is a defense. Ask yourself,

"What am I afraid of hearing? What am I afraid would happen to me if I just listened and didn't respond?"

You may realize that maybe you won't get to say your side. You may realize that you're afraid that you'll become a doormat. Maybe you're afraid that you may find you were wrong about what you are arguing about. If the feelings get too intense, ask your partner if you could share these fears with him/her.

When Stav and I get into an argument, once we get past the initial insanity and we're willing to listen to each other, we take turns talking. One person will talk until there is nothing else to say and the other just listens. No comments. No interruptions. No defense. This does not mean that this is a dump session. When practicing defenselessness, **both** sides must agree to be defenseless. The person talking is not allowed to verbally attack or dump on the other person. You are not allowed to heap abuse on the other party (no matter how much *you think* he/she warrants it). For example, attacking statements such as, "You are a big, fat slob" or "You're a loser in bed" are not appropriate. They only bring up more defense in the other person. The purpose of this exercise is to get both sides to listen. This also means that **both** sides will get to share.

It is very helpful for the speaker to use "I" statements instead of "You" statements. For example, saying, "You are always late and inconsiderate. You don't care about me," sets up a feeling of blame and puts your partner on the defensive. By communicating *your feelings*, as *you experience* them, you take the pressure off the other person and place the focus on you: "*I feel* angry whenever you are late. It makes me feel unloved and not important in your life. It reminds me of how my father treated me."

You have to remember that in any situation, it is *your reaction* to what the other person is doing that is part of the problem. Seeing and expressing your reaction lets each party see that there is more going on than meets the eye.

We also need to remember that our own perceptions may be wrong. What we do is make decisions and judgements based on what we believe we are seeing – and most of the time we are wrong. A typical, blamed-based argument may start with,

"You never care about me! When I got home tonight you just ignored me. You really love your newspaper more than me!"

Once again, this kind of interaction only sets up more blame and defense. So another powerful phrase we have found to use is,

"My perception is. . ."

"My perception is that when I got home, you seemed to not know I was here. I felt ignored and unimportant. My perception is that you seemed more interested in reading the paper than in connecting with me."

What this communicates to your partner is that this is how *you see* the situation. This is how *you interpret* his actions. It may or may not be the right interpretation, but at least the receiver now knows how his/her actions are being perceived.

A couple in my office were sharing, when suddenly the man accused his wife of not really listening to him because she had an intense, but distant, look on her face. I could see her immediately tense up in defense. I supported her in taking a breath, and I asked him to rephrase his comment, using the "I feel" and "My perception is" statements.

"I feel angry right now," he said. "My perception of you is that you are not really listening to me and I feel ignored."

When he shared his feelings responsibly and told her that it was *his* perception, she visibly relaxed. When he asked for her feedback she replied,

"Well, actually I had some fear about what you may share, so maybe I was a little withdrawn. But that intense look on my face was that I was really trying to listen! This is really new for me!"

Just plain listening and being defenseless will initially make many of us feel fearful, like the woman in this example. If you have a lot of fear before a sharing session, it helps to imagine that you are protected in an invisible raincoat. A shield that allows communication back and forth, but does not allow abuse or hurt to enter.

When the speaker is finished talking, the other person takes a few breaths to help digest what was just said. Sometimes I repeat back to Stav what she has just said. This insures that what *I think* I heard was indeed what she said. If I am wrong, she corrects it and I repeat what she said until I get it right. The purpose of this is not to parrot back what was said, but to *truly understand* where the speaker is coming from. It also gives the speaker the feeling that they were actually listened to and understood.

I find that when I let myself listen, without trying to develop a defense, I really hear her! Not just her words but also the emotions—the unspoken hurt and anger. I begin to feel what she is feeling. I may not agree with the feelings, but I begin to understand where she is coming from.

Then, it's my turn to talk. I may still be angry or hurt, but I remember that this is now **my** time to tell my side. Without attack. Without making anybody wrong. When I am finished talking, she takes a few breaths, and may now have more to say. We continue this, alternating telling our sides, until we feel that there is nothing left to tell. Usually, we start with explaining how we are feeling angry, but after a few sentences, we tell each other our hurts, and finally, the argument shifts when we share our fears. Admitting to each other what we are afraid of is the most defenseless act we can commit. When we do that, we are showing our partner a part of ourselves that can be *perceived* as weakness and risking whether the other person will still honor us.

When we are defenseless, we are, in effect, saying, "I really don't know all the answers. I *think* I know, but I am *willing* to see something better." When we lower our defenses, we are in a position to learn, we are in a position to grow, we are in a position to find happiness.

It takes great willingness and courage to be defenseless enough to change our minds. It takes great willingness and courage to be willing to see another person's side. It takes great willingness and courage to remember that whenever we are having an argument, that both people are 100% correct—in their perception. Being defenseless allows us the opportunity to see through the other person's eyes. We have spent too many years being right and unhappy. We have been like the old, crabby curmudgeon, who, when asked what he wanted for breakfast, replied,

"Two eggs. One boiled. One scrambled."

After his wife made the two eggs as ordered, he proceeded to eat only one of them.

"Why didn't you eat the other egg?" she asked.

"Because you scrambled the wrong one," grumbled her husband.

It's time for us to start making *being happy* our priority in life. And if we have to feel a little embarrassed along the way—so what? If at times you have to eat crow, I find a dash of humor tenderizes it a lot.

One time, Stav and I were fighting over whether to buy a certain flower vase for our house. We were just beginning to make some headway financially and she wanted to decorate the house a little. But I needed to purchase a new tape recorder to replace the one I used to record my classes, and I was in a lot of fear around whether we had enough money. The vase didn't even cost that much—about $30, but in my controlling way, I could not justify the expense for both items. And so, we fought and argued. I finally got so furious that I stormed out of the house, to buy my recorder.

As I sat in my car and put the key into the ignition slot, something just told me that running away was stupid. My ego wanted to be right, but I knew that if I persisted in my actions, I would definitely ruin the rest of the day—possibly a few days. For what? For $30? So grudgingly, I trudged back into the house.

"Look," I told Stav, "I'd rather be with you and hate you than be right and alone. So let's go get my *damn* recorder and then we'll look at those *stupid* vases."

Stav hopped off the couch with a smile and we went on our way. A block down the street, she turned to me and said, "You know, I love how you are always willing to change. I just love you."

Her comment softened the moment and I found myself smiling, in spite of my fears and anger, and then we burst out laughing. Our defenses dropped and we felt connected again, which is the gift of surrendering. It restores joy and a sense of humor.

"We don't **have** to get a vase," she said, "but I just want to look at them again to see if we even like them."

The ironic thing about the whole story, is that when we both looked at the vases, neither of us totally liked the $30 vase, but we both felt drawn to an elegant Mikasa vase that cost three times as much. We ended up buying what we both really liked. Funny, how the money was no longer the issue once I relinquished control.

And you know what? When I thought back, I remembered that when we first looked at the vases, *three days before*, I remembered thinking then, that what I *really* wanted was that particular vase. The fight wasn't with Stav. I was the one afraid that I would spend more money. And then I tried to blame Stav for it. To this day, whenever I see that vase, I thank God we bought it. It looks wonderful and is an affirmation that I, too, deserve nice things in my life. It affirms that I can stretch just a little bit, that it is safe to change my mind. I don't need to defend myself, my money or my pride.

*A Course in Miracles* says that what we are really afraid of, what we really defend against is—love. As we learn to lower our defenses, to trust that we are not so horrible inside, to laugh at our insanity instead of protecting it, what we find—is love.

When we surrender to the love of God, when we surrender to the love of others, when we allow our defenses to go down, life gets sweeter and easier.

# Self Discovery Quiz

- *Which is harder? Admitting you're wrong or trying to pretend you are always right?*

- *Have you ever persisted in a fight, even though you realized you were in the wrong? Why? How long did it take before the truth finally got out? Or, did the truth finally ever get out?*

- *If you are defenseless, are you afraid your partner will run over you?*

- *If your partner was defenseless, would you run over him/her?*

- *Can you be trusted to tell your truth and state your true feelings even when you are mistaken? If not, how can others be defenseless with you?*

- *When you grew up, did you always have to defend yourself? From whom? Do you still act as if you need to defend yourself?*

- *Do you feel that you have to defend yourself at home or at work? From whom do you need to defend yourself? What are you afraid they will do?*

- *Have you ever tried to see another person's side to an issue and been won over? Was it so bad?*

*Be certain any answer to a problem
the Holy Spirit solves
will always be one in which no one loses.*
**A Course in Miracles** Text pg. 501 / 539

*Often the best way to win is
to forget to keep score.*
Marianne Espinosa Murphy

*A man should never be ashamed to own
he has been in the wrong,
which is but saying,
in other words, that he is wiser today
than he was yesterday.*
Alexander Pope

*Is it not possible that
all your problems have been solved,
but you have removed yourself
from the solution?*
**A Course in Miracles** Text pg. 342 / 368

# Nobody Has To Lose

Have you ever spent endless hours trying to convince your partner that your point of view or what you want is the right thing for both of you? Have you ever sold out to your partner to let them have their way, just to keep the peace, only to find yourself feeling resentful towards your partner for getting their way? These scenarios are very typical variations of what happens in relationships when we get stuck in power and control and insist that only one person can win in an argument.

A conscious, healthy relationship, on the other hand, is one that believes in a win-win solution *in all cases*. No one has to lose in order for the other person to get what they want. This is the highest stage in a relationship; it is called synergy.

To reach synergy it is imperative that we open up to the wisdom that is within each of us. It is also imperative that we open up to the wisdom of God. When Stav and I have a disagreement, we no longer try to solve it ourselves (OK! We do try to do it ourselves—for awhile.) But when we finally get calm and centered, we offer the problem up to God. We tell ourselves that there is no problem too big that God in us cannot solve. We tell ourselves and each other that there is an answer that will make *both* of us happy, and that there is a Highest Thought that will support the growth and happiness of both of us. We tell ourselves and each other that we want a win-win in this situation, that is, Stav can win and feel good about the outcome, *and* I can win and feel good about the outcome.

Just stating the fact that there is an answer that will satisfy both sides, starts the process of healing, because it concentrates the power of our minds towards formulating an answer, as opposed to wasting that power trying to convince our partner that they are wrong. Surrendering the problem to God now allows our minds to be open to new ideas and possibilities. The answer may come in a day, a week, a month. Stav and I have learned to relax and trust that God will always help us to find a solution. And any solution that God provides always makes both of us feel as if we have won.

When you are willing to create a win-win situation, the world will open up and show you possibilities. After my second divorce, my ex-wife, Peggy, moved back to Chicago with my four-year-old daughter, Mary Jean. A few months later I decided to fly out and visit my daughter. I talked to Peggy over the phone about my plans, explaining that I wanted Mary Jean to stay overnight with me. Peggy said that she didn't think that it would be a good idea, since they had just moved to Chicago and Mary Jean was still settling in. I got angry and defensive, feeling that Peggy was using my guilt to control me and my visit. I told her that I didn't agree and resented that she was controlling. We ended the conversation unresolved, upset and angry.

I stewed in my resentment for a few days until it occurred to me to call my friend, Donna, for support. She asked,

"Do you want to be right or happy about this? Do you want to force your daughter to be with you if she's not ready to stay overnight?"

"No," I replied, "I just want to spend time with her, but I feel that Peggy is just guilt tripping me to get her way. She's making me pay for leaving her."

"Well, Jerry, why don't you leave the decision up to your daughter? Why don't you let her decide?"

That was an answer I had never considered. I called Peggy and asked if it would be all right if we let the decision rest on Mary Jean. She immediately said that it was OK with her. Suddenly, all the tension around the situation eased. I saw that Peggy wasn't trying to punish me, she was just looking out for Mary Jean's welfare. I was the one projecting my own guilty feelings into the argument.

When I went to Chicago later that week, Mary Jean initially said that she did not want to stay overnight with me. I felt hurt, but I let it be OK. Then two days later, at a party for my grandmother, she changed her mind and said she wanted to spend the rest of the time with me—and stay with me overnight. When I called Peggy, I was surprised how supportive she actually was. When I took Mary Jean back that night, Peggy had her things packed and there was no hassle.

When you ask God for a win-win, you are finally surrendering what you **think** is right to a higher power that **knows** what is right. You are actually saying that you truly do not know your own best interests and that you want God to help.

As I stated earlier in this book, getting to the win-win scenario will take you through every step—*Individuality, Competition, Compromise, Cooperation* and *Synergy*. Asking for a win-win confronts our ego and our pride, because what we are actually doing is humbly admitting that we don't *know* what is best for us and all concerned. We are admitting that, if we are fighting over something, there must be an area that we need to heal. Remember that we create our world through our thoughts. If you believe that a certain situation is unsolvable, what do you think you will create *by the very power of your thoughts*? The situation being unsolvable! It is our own thoughts that keep us trapped.

When you change your mind about the argument, when you both agree that there **is** an answer and you **will** find it—with God's help, you have channeled the power of your minds towards finding the answer. You need to know, though, that when you commit to finding an answer that will work for both of you, you may end up changing your minds about what you originally wanted, but the ultimate answer will always be one that both of you will *still feel good about*.

Many times we get stuck in wanting something to look a certain way, when all the while, another way would make us equally, if not more, happy. Sometimes, even though it may hurt us, we just want our way because of years of being deprived. Watch what happens in divorce court when both parties **want their way**, even if it means using up all of their money and assets to get it.

Getting to a win-win requires that we be willing to see that maybe there is more going on than just the issue we see. Maybe there are old, unacknowledged hurts and fears triggering our words and desires. As *A Course in Miracles* says,

> *You are never upset for the reason you think.*
>
> *Workbook Lesson 5*

Although this quote for the *Course* is referring to our being upset for originally thinking we had separated ourselves from God, it really applies to any upset in our lives. For me, the *very idea* that there could be another cause to my problems was liberating, although a little unsettling as well.

Early in our marriage, when money was quite tight, Stav went to a sale and spent $75 for two designer dresses. I hit the roof! How could she squander all that money when we could hardly pay our bills? Naturally, we got into a big fight. What I saw was an irresponsible woman, buying things for herself, and what she saw was a tight, controlling man who didn't want his wife to have anything.

Finally, after a few days of cold anger, we decided we needed help, and we called our friend Nancy to support us.

"So what do you guys want here?" she said. "Is it time to end this marriage? Is that it?"

"No," we said, "we don't want to end our marriage. We just feel stuck around this money issue."

"Do you want a win-win here?"

We had totally forgotten about that possibility. Once we agreed that we wanted each person to feel good about the outcome, our hearts began to shift. Suddenly, I wanted Stav to feel good! I didn't want her to feel guilty or bad about giving to herself, but I was afraid of not having enough money.

"Jerry," started Stav, "I am not a spendthrift. I have been a single mother for four years. I've run a home and I have helped put my daughters through college. In all those years, I have never gone bankrupt. I have never bounced a check. I have never been financially irresponsible. Do you really think I am that stupid?"

"I just get scared about the money. All I see is the bills and then you go out and spend $75 for dresses."

At this point, Stav and Nancy informed me (once again) that the cost for those dresses at regular price would have been $400 to $500.

"Look, I know you've run a household and that you're better at it than I am, but I'm afraid of being out of control. I'm afraid of you spending all our money."

"Jerry, stop making me pay for the mistakes you've made in your past relationships. I'm not them!"

As we talked, it became obvious that what I was reacting to was my fear of being out of control, and she was reacting to her fear of being controlled. She grew up in poverty and her father controlled the purse strings.

Then Stav said something that clicked:

"You know, Jerry, I don't even think this has anything to do with the money. Seventy-five dollars is not that much. I think that you're just resentful because you never give yourself anything. You scrimp on yourself and then resent me for giving to myself. I'm willing to take the dresses back, but I don't think that that will solve the problem."

I felt my body go *Zing* as she said that and I knew there was an element of truth. So far, in our marriage, God had always come through. Even though we were in fear, somehow the money always appeared. Stav trusted God more than I did. She knew that at times we need to give to ourselves, that wearing a nice dress or jacket is a loving reminder that we do deserve more than a drudge-filled life.

I was so busy scrimping and worrying that I hardly ever gave anything nice to myself. I felt angry, at myself, God and Stav. And I resented any time that Stav gave to herself.

And so, with the help of Nancy, we came to an agreement. Since I had such resistance to giving to myself, and since Stav was a reflection of the part of my mind that *wanted* to give to myself, we agreed that whenever she bought herself something I had to go out and spend the same amount of money on myself. So, that weekend we went out and she selected some silk shirts and ties (on sale, of course). I had never worn silk. In fact I thought it was too feminine. But you know what? I *liked* how it felt. And until I got comfortable with the act of taking care of myself, I followed the agreement, no matter what. Whenever she bought something, I went out and bought myself something also.

The money? Don't ask me. Somehow we created more than enough. Somehow God always came through, showing us that there was enough money to pay the bills **and** take care of our desires. I have since learned what a wonderful teacher Stav is. She opened me up to trusting her more, to trusting God more and to finally giving myself the things I liked.

There is no problem that can stand up to the combined will of two people and God. Arguments about money, bills, sex, kids, or food stand no chance when addressed honestly and responsibly with a determination to find a win-win. Make a new agreement with yourself right now. Commit to always finding the answer in which nobody ever has to lose again. You'll be happier, and so will the world.

# Affirmations

- *There is no problem too big for God.*

- *I now let the wisdom of the Universe show me possibilities.*

- *I **can** change my mind. I now expect a miracle.*

- *I now ask my partner for help in solving our problems.*

- *God is also within my partner and so I know he/she is trustworthy.*

- *Deep within myself and my partner is the answer we seek.*

- *I now put myself in a place where I can receive the answers I need.*

- *Even in my darkest hour I can win. I no longer let temporary situations determine my faith.*

- *I am determined to be happy.*

- *My goal is to get back to the love I want to feel for my partner. I now let nothing stand in the way.*

- *Out of infinite possibilities, I now know that there is an answer that can satisfy me and my partner.*

- *When I let God be on our side, I am in the majority.*

*If You Want Guarantees, Buy a Toaster*
**Book title by Robert M. Hochheiser**

*Trust in God, but tether your camel.*
**Arab Proverb**

*A chip on the shoulder is too heavy a piece of baggage to carry through life.*
**B. C. Forbes**

*I'd trust other people more if only I knew myself less.*
**Anonymous**

*If we only listened to our intellect, we'd never have a love affair. We'd never have a friendship. We'd never go into business, because we'd be cynical. Well, that's nonsense. You've got to jump off cliffs all the time and build your wings on the way down.*
**Ray Bradbury**

# In God We Trust
# – Oh, Sure!

A healthy sense of trust is a crucial ingredient to any successful relationship. Without trust, no relationship will ever succeed. When we don't trust, we live in fear, our heart is closed off and the world is a scary place. But without trust, the world as we know it would stop cold.

Whether you feel that you trust others or not, you already trust more than you realize. Just for a moment, imagine a world without trust. You couldn't write a check, because how could anyone trust that you had funds to cover it? Credit cards would be obsolete, since nobody would be trustworthy enough to pay what they owed. You would have to grow your own food because you could not trust the markets to sell healthy items. Nobody would drive because you could not trust that anyone would honor a red light. There would be no mail service since nobody could trust that the mail would be delivered or even sent to the correct person. Houses would become armed camps—fortresses against our untrustworthy neighbors. A world without trust would indeed be a cold, cold world.

So why has trust gotten such a bad rap in relationships? It's because we demand *guarantees* and unwavering loyalty. We demand absolute security in a changing world. We expect every relationship to be 100% trustworthy, like the Post Office—there through rain, or sleet, or snow. This is unrealistic.

Clients will come to me and tell me their stories of how they trusted someone and then were let down. So they decide to never trust another person again. "People are just not dependable!" they complain.

But let me ask you, have you ever had a power failure? Did you stop using electricity because it has failed you in the past? Have you ever had a pen run out of ink in the middle of a paper? Stopped using pens lately? Has your car ever broken down? Have you quit using your car? We base our lives on undependable objects that may break down or stop at any time, and yet we continue using them anyway.

Now I realize that there is a lot more emotion invested in a relationship than in a pen that runs out of ink or a broken car, but the principle is still the same. Relationships, jobs, cars, pens, electricity are all tools in this world. We use those things to extend our love and learn about ourselves. They are not the ends but the means to finding out about ourselves. When you find a pen that doesn't deliver, you look for one that does. If your car repeatedly breaks down, you replace it with one that runs. You find what works, but you don't stop using the article.

So too with relationships. I see people who swear that they will never get into another relationship because they were disappointed or hurt instead of realizing that maybe they had a part in the upset. Instead of finding how to create a healthy, loving relationship, they just give up. And then they get to feel lonely and abandoned.

But how many people hold onto unhealthy relationships, because they are afraid of change, are afraid to be alone or are just stuck in a toxic pattern?

Some people believe that a relationship should be based on blind trust. This is *really* asking for trouble. I have known people who got hurt after trusting another person, and that the trust was based upon the fact that the person was Christian or that they went to the "right" church, or that they read *A Course in Miracles*. Trust is not guaranteed because of the church you go to or because you and your partner have the same reading preferences.

Trust is not guaranteed by an engagement ring, a marriage license, or wedding vows. Healthy trust is **earned**—over time, as each person *demonstrates* his/her own trustworthiness. To paraphrase the E. F. Hutton commercial, "We make trust the old-fashioned way. We *earn it.*"

When I get a new client, I do not expect them to trust me. In fact, *I don't want them to trust me*. People who trust blindly have not learned how to set healthy boundaries and will repeatedly create situations that violate their trust and spirit. Actually, not trusting is part of the development of a *healthy* relationship. I want a new client to listen to my guidance and test it out. I want them to experience, one step at a time, that I can be trusted and, most importantly, that *their* inner guidance can also be trusted.

The first person we need to learn to trust is ourselves. People who do not trust others are actually untrusting of themselves. I was once working with a client as she cried over her latest disappointment.

"How could he just hurt me like that! I trusted him and he just used me!"

She continued on in this vein for quite some time. After she settled down a bit and was able to see the situation through different eyes, I asked her,

"When you first got into a relationship with him, how did you feel?"

"Well, I felt really excited and in love, but there was also something in my heart that said that something was not right."

As we talked further, she got to see that she had not trusted her first instincts. She had not trusted the feeling that he was pushing too hard, too fast and that she needed more time. She began to see that she needed to develop a sense of trust with her heart.

In his book *A Path with Heart*, Jack Kornfield gives the example of a spiritual teacher who told his students to never trust him blindly, that it was necessary to also check in with their own beliefs.

"What if," the guru said, "one night, unbeknownst to you, I had a small stroke that affected my mind? And what if I began to make outrageous claims or demands on you? What if I asked you to do things that were immoral or unethical? Would you do them? I hope not. I hope you would trust yourselves enough to get *me* help. Just because I'm a teacher does not mean that I cannot make a mistake."

Having blind trust for another is irresponsible and a sign of spiritual immaturity. Having blind trust is, in effect, saying, "You know more than I do and you will take care of me. I don't want to take responsibility for my thoughts, feelings, and actions, so you do it for me." There is only one entity that we can blindly trust, and that is God. But truly trusting God only comes *after* learning to trust your inner voice (which is God), and then practicing, step-by-step, trusting others.

As children, many of us had our trust broken. We were needy, weak and inexperienced, and those older than us may have lied to us, taken advantage of us, or abused us, physically, mentally or emotionally. We grow up with unexpressed anger at those who hurt us. We may even have caught our parents lying to others, which then taught us that people don't mean what they say and can be deceitful.

But growing up and healthily relating to others requires that we let go of these old hurts and make a new, mature choice—a choice for life. You see, as an adult, you now have *the power* and *responsibility* to decide all over again what it is you want. We have to "call back our spirit," to quote Caroline Myss. This is where, with all the anger, hurt, rage, joy and maturity, we claim back our lives, claim back all the energy we waste protecting ourselves and claim back all the energy we waste obsessing over the past. We begin to say to our past abusers, "No more! It stops here and now! No more will I allow this behavior to occur!"

So, how do you develop trust within yourself? Have you ever had an experience in which what you were being told did not agree with what you felt inside? Did you, as I have done many times, do what felt easier in the moment instead of trusting that warning voice? Maybe you had sex, for example, when you were not ready, because it was easier than standing up for your personal ideals or asking for more time. And later you regret it.

Listning to the inner voice is a *first step* and a major one. It takes time and practice, but as you do, as you build one experience upon another, the voice gets stronger and more credible. As *A Course in Miracles* says,

> *The Holy Spirit's voice is as loud as your willingness to listen.* **Text pg. 145 / 157**

Another step in developing trust is to take an inventory of all the areas where you are not trustworthy—where have you lied, cheated or stole? In other words, how have you been out of integrity? You may not be a bank robber or a jewel thief, but where do you steal time from your employer? Where do you lie to your partner? Even white lies? Where do you *stretch* the truth? I am not saying that you have to be squeaky clean, but stop projecting onto others what you yourself also do. A major reason for not trusting others is that we unconsciously project our own untrustworthiness onto them. As you clean up your own issues and get in integrity with yourself, you will discover that the world is more trustworthy than you originally perceived.

You can then develop trust for others—once again—step-by-step. When I wanted to stop living unconsciously, it was necessary for me to trust a teacher who would tell me the truth, whether I liked it or not. He would give me exercises and affirmations to do that I thought were crazy, but even though my ego screamed in defiance, my inner voice kept saying, "I know you're scared here, but this is safe." This was not blind trust, though. This was trust with both eyes open. I questioned and fought back, but always with the feeling that I wanted to know the truth about myself, not just to be right.

# Regaining Trust after a Betrayal

So let's take a particularly painful example. You have just found that your lover has been having an affair. He/she is repentant and doesn't want the relationship to end. Will you take him/her back?

This is where trust and responsibility meet. First, allow yourself to truly feel your feelings of betrayal, hurt and anger. Too many times I see partners "forgive" an errant mate too soon while leaving the unresolved feelings simmering inside. Learn to trust the process of just naturally feeling your emotions. Though you may be initially afraid that these feelings will never subside, trust me when I say that they will. And they can be powerful friends in showing you where you went wrong and what your next step should be.

While allowing yourself to feel, I also *strongly* suggest getting into counseling. There will be lots of painful feelings to be released and new areas to be explored. You will feel paranoid and suspicious for quite some time. In spite of these feelings, healing can still occur. But you need a sane voice, like a counselor, someone outside the drama, to give you clarity and to guide the process. Professional advice, especially from someone who specializes in emotional release and infidelity issues can help determine your next step. A qualified counselor can help determine whether the affair was a one-time occurrence, with a need to more deeply explore intimacy issues in the relationship, of if it's a hidden pattern coming to light, such as a sexual addiction.

After awhile, with the help of your counselor, you can begin to take responsibility for *your part* in the experience. This process is not about assigning blame and pointing fingers. And it is not about letting the perpetrator off the hook, who still has his/her issues to heal. In some cases I have seen a clever perpetrator who is able to twist things around so much that the wronged party actually begins to take on all the blame.

So when you are ready to look at your part, ask yourself, "Before I found out about this affair, did I have a clue (sometimes there aren't any) that something was going on? Were there hints that *I chose* to ignore? Did I allow him/her to convince me there was nothing going on when all the time I *felt* differently? Where did I not trust myself?" Have a lot of compassion for yourself when you do this process. Remember the state of mind you were in at the time and accept and love yourself for where you were. But also look for the clues. Look for where you chose not to address any issues. This allows you to stop being a victim and to claim back your life as a living, breathing, powerful person, who *chose* not to look at issues that were painful. And from this point you can learn from your mistakes and deepen your relationships with others.

After some assistance to clarify the issues and some time to make an informed decision, if you decide to take him/her back, do it responsibly — with both eyes open. You can do it with the thought, "I now choose to take you back and I take 100% responsibility for my choice. If you are not trustworthy, I expect to learn sooner than I did in the past. I will listen to my heart. If you *are* trustworthy, I am willing to let you **earn** my trust once again."

And if your trust is broken again, you need to trust yourself and take full responsibility for ending the relationship. There will be fears and doubts, but learn to trust your inner voice and strength. And continue to get help and counseling.

In the movie *Excalibur*, there is a scene of trust and surrender that really speaks to me. Young Arthur has pulled the sword, Excalibur, from the stone, and half of the knights join and proclaim him king. The other half reject him, saying he is a bastard or some sort of trick that Merlin the magician is trying to foist off on them. The rebel knights attack the castle of one of Arthur's allies, and Arthur joins the battle against the rebel knights.

During the fight, Arthur ambushes Sir Uriens, the leader of the rebels, unhorsing him and bringing him down into the river. Arthur grabs Uriens, holding Excalibur to his neck, yelling,

"Surrender your arms and swear allegiance to me! I need battle lords like you."

Sir Uriens screams back, "I'll never swear allegiance to a squire!"

And Arthur is stopped.

"You're right," he says. "I am not yet a knight." And Arthur pulls the sword away from his enemy's throat, reverses it and hands Excalibur to Uriens.

"So you, Uriens, will knight me. And then, knight to knight, you can swear allegiance to me." Arthur then kneels before him in the river waiting to be knighted.

Uriens holds the sword, the sword of power, the sword that whoever wields it will rule England. And he is torn. Some of the other rebel knights shout to him to keep it. His arms shake as he tries to decide whether to kill this upstart boy or knight him.

Then, Uriens performs the knighting ritual, tapping each shoulder and proclaiming Arthur a knight and giving him the right to bear arms. As Uriens finishes the act, he falls at Arthur's feet and claims his eternal loyalty.

"Never have I seen such courage! The blood that flows in your veins must surely be from Uther Pendragon (the first king of England and Arthur's father)."

At the end of the scene, Merlin, the magician who can see the future, is shown mumbling to himself, "I never saw *this* before."

Trusting goes against all logic because it is from the heart. It is not a commodity to be traded. It is a gift to yourself and others.

We cannot have a healthy relationship without trust, but we must first nurture it within ourselves. We must practice listening to that still small voice that will never lead us wrong. As we practice, we get stronger and our lives and relationships are more successful.

*A Course in Miracles* says,

> *Who would attempt to fly with the tiny wings of a sparrow when the mighty power of eagles have been given him?*     **Teacher's Manual pg. 9 / 9**

Learn to trust yourself. Become a trustworthy person by practicing integrity in all your doings. And by becoming more trustworthy, you will discover that you are attracting more trustworthy people to you. And then you can learn to trust God and learn to trust others. And in doing so, you too will fly—with the mighty power of eagles.

# *Affirmations*

- *I can now trust others because I now trust myself.*
- *When I am not trusting, I only need to look inside myself to acknowledge and heal my fear.*
- *God will never drop me on my head. I am always cradled in the loving arms of God.*
- *I am opening my heart to the truth about myself and others.*
- *I am now an adult and now take responsibility for the experiences I choose to have.*
- *I am now an adult and choose no longer to be fooled by others.*
- *I can ask for advice and support, but I now know that the final decision is always up to me. I no longer expect others to fix my life.*
- *I now allow myself the time to make decisions.*

*If you always tell the truth,*
*you don't have to remember anything.*
**Mark Twain**

*When friends stop being*
*frank and useful to each other,*
*the whole world loses some of its radiance.*
**Anatole Broyard**

*There are chapters in every life*
*which are seldom read and*
*certainly not aloud.*
**Carol Shields**

*Do not always assume that the other fellow*
*has intelligence equal to yours.*
*He may have more.*
**Terry Thomas**

*What we need is more people who*
*specialize in the impossible.*
**Theodore Roethke**

# Stop Playing
## *"I've Got a Secret"*

A *Course in Miracles* states that all the Holy Spirit wants is for us to bring our secrets to Him, because that is where true healing begins. We all have secrets that we are ashamed of. We have secrets about what we have done wrong in the past. We have secrets about what others have done to us. We have secret thoughts and judgments about others. We have secret sexual fantasies, secret hates and secret loves. We have secret judgments about our bodies that we hope nobody will ever know.

Holding onto secrets only causes pain. Do you realize how much energy goes into keeping secrets, defending outright lies and white lies, and how much denial and defense is needed?

The movie *The Prince of Tides* presents a great example of the destruction caused by secrets. Not only are the children kept in pain by not letting the family secret out, but even the mother uses secrets to control them. She tells the son that she loves him more than his sister and then tells him not to let her know because it would hurt her feelings. It's their "little secret". And throughout his adolescence, the boy feels guilty for being loved more than his sister. Years later, when he finally tells his sister, she laughs and tells him that Mom did the same thing to her and for years *she* felt guilty.

Secrets are insidious. They are one of the biggest tools used by the ego to keep our sense of separation from each other in place. Secrets keep us separate from our lovers, our families, from God and, most importantly, from ourselves. Therapy is basically a fact-finding mission for secrets, because even though there are many secrets that we are not aware of, we still feel guilty and controlled by them.

When we bring our secrets to the light of day, by exposing ourselves to God's love or the love of our relationships, there is always a moment of fear, a thought that we'll be rejected. However, I have seen many times where once the secret was told, and the fears aired and tears cried, the relationship got stronger. There was a deeper bonding.

I had two clients who were in a relationship. They both loved each other but were also very afraid of getting too close. Their pattern was to get close, feel scared of their intimacy, have a fight, separate, miss each other and make up, and get close once again, get scared again, have a fight, separate, etc. They were playing a game that my friend, Rev. Lura Smedstad, calls *slap-and-tickle*. What they would do was when the intimacy got too scary, they would *slap* the other person to push them away. But then, the perpetrator felt lonely and missed the other person, so he/she would *tickle* and entice the hurt person back into intimacy, until the intimacy got too scary again. Have you ever played this game? I have. It's maddening, and nothing ever gets accomplished.

Anyway, this couple was working with me on their relationship. They were learning various relationship tools and learning how to tell each other the emotional truth. After a few sessions, Harry lost his job, and Jane, who was increasingly unhappy about her present job, decided to check out the jobs in San Francisco. Harry had been looking for a job in Monterey, but, so far, had found nothing. A few weeks later, Jane got a job offer in the San Francisco area and accepted it. Naturally, Harry started to look for a job in San Francisco, but nothing seemed to happen.

Finally, in one session, I asked Harry if he really believed that his thoughts create. He said yes, and then I asked what thoughts were keeping him from creating a job in San Francisco. He replied that he couldn't imagine what they were.

"You know, Harry," I said, "every time you mention moving to San Francisco, my body goes 'thud.' I don't get it. I know you *want* to be there, but I think there is something more going on. There is something you're not telling yourself that's stopping you from fully committing to this move."

Well, neither of us was aware of what was going on, and so the two of us floundered for a few minutes, trying to grasp what the unspoken, secret thoughts were. Then I had an idea.

"You said earlier that Monterey was *originally* your first choice. That was where **you** wanted to move to from the beginning."

"That's right."

"And now you're moving to San Francisco because Jane is going there. Not because it's *your* choice, but because Jane is now moving there."

"Yessss," he said, slowly beginning to feel something move.

"So, how does it *feel*, to be a man, without a job and *following* your woman across the United States?"

Suddenly, he became aware of his own, hidden low self-esteem. He began to tell himself the truth of how he didn't feel like a man and how it felt to follow his woman to another city. It made him feel weak and unlovable, and it made him feel like he was a leech.

"You know, Jerry, I'm afraid to tell her that even though San Francisco wasn't my first choice, I want to go there *because I love her*, because I want to be with her. But I don't want her to feel as if she has to take care of me or that she's responsible for me."

As soon as he said that, I felt the room lighten up! Finally, he was telling himself some truths! He actually began to smile, and now I could actually feel excited about him moving to San Francisco.

"So," I said, "can you tell Jane that you will take full responsibility for *your* experience in San Francisco? That you don't *know* whether the relationship will work out or not, but that you want to be with her anyway and that she owes you nothing?"

"Yes, I can," he replied as he took a deep breath and let himself feel that. "You know, I've been afraid to tell her because she might get scared and end the relationship."

"So, which is better, Harry, not telling her and living on pins and needles, or letting her know *exactly* how you feel and then feeling what comes up?"

The look on Harry's face changed. He no longer felt internally torn between his opposing secret thoughts. He had brought them to light and now, at least, knew there was something he could do. He looked lighter and happier, and he told me so. He felt free.

That night Harry told Jane how he really felt, why he was willing to move to San Francisco. When he told her that he just wanted to be with her, she replied, "Well, I want you to be there, also. I want you with me. I'm scared around our relationship, too, but I want you there anyway. I was afraid to say anything because I didn't want to force you to move if you didn't want to."

As soon as Harry exposed himself to his secret thoughts and fears, the fears disappeared. Once he recognized that moving to San Francisco was not his idea but that he was following Jane anyway, he saw that it didn't matter. Once he recognized that it was his own conflicting fears of his masculinity and what it meant to be a man, he saw that it didn't matter whether he followed her or she followed him. What was important was to tell the truth and commit to the love—no matter how it felt.

As Stav and I tell people about our intensive Six-Month Program, "No corner will be left undusted." It is the fear we have about what people may think if we tell our secrets that keeps us defensive and scared. But I have seen people tell their most "horrendous secrets" and nobody reacts to it at all. It's almost anticlimactic. This person is shaking in his boots as he relates how, for example, he spent time in prison, and the other people in the group kind of look at him with a "so what" expression. Their response is usually, "So you went to prison for such and such. Am I supposed to reject you now?" What the others respect and admire is the courage it took to tell the secret. What the secret *is* never matters. It's the release of the suppressed energy of trying to hold onto the secret that brings relief.

Revealing our secrets is not like going to confession. It's not about relating all of our *sins*, hoping that we may be forgiven. It's also not about telling all to all. We need to exercise good judgment about who and where to disclose our secrets.

But opening up is an opportunity to be defenseless. It is process of unveiling what we always thought was unlovable about us and being willing to see it with new eyes. It's about giving us an opportunity to forgive ourselves. It's about giving us an opportunity to see that other people will not judge us and spurn our love.

Early on in a relationship many people will relate how they were alcoholics, divorced, did drugs, etc.—usually in an effort to see whether the other person will stick around. That's the easy part! Tell yourself the truth. Aren't you just a little bit proud of all the rotten things you did? Isn't there just a little pride around what you survived, what hazards you overcame and how far down you went? Isn't there a little rascal that enjoyed being a brat, even though you may regret what you did?

However, the really hard secrets are the *little things*. The little things that we ourselves do not want to see—how we shut our feelings down when we get afraid, how we control, how we judge, how angry we get when somebody does not listen to our wishes, how childish we can act, how we leave the toilet seat up in unconscious resentment and control.

For years I considered myself to be a liberal male. I *said* I believed in equal rights and pay for men and women. I *really believed* that I believed that men and women were equal. However, in my Six Month Program, I began to see my secret self. Though I said the right words, I actually treated women as second-class citizens. I secretly thought that I was better than they were. I secretly thought that I was smarter than them. It felt like a slap on the face when my teacher, Joe, confronted me with the fact that I was a "Male Chauvinist Pig!"

However, when I looked at those secret thoughts, when I honestly looked at how I treated women, I saw he was right. I began to see why my relationships failed. I had the right words and acts to fool a woman into being with me, but, over time, they began to see my secret thoughts. When they confronted me, I always denied it, thinking that they were paranoid. Ultimately, we would break up and my secrets would remain safe.

As Joe confronted me, I suddenly remembered an incident in my first marriage. My first wife, Marge, wanted to go to college, and I wholeheartedly supported her. I helped her find a school and helped her with studying for the entrance exams. But when she passed those entrance exams and was actually accepted into college, I went nuts. I felt threatened and went crazy with fear. You see, I secretly never *expected* her to pass those tests. I secretly thought she wasn't smart enough. I was terrified of her going to college, where she might meet a man more handsome than me, smarter than me or richer than me. And so, even though I was *supporting* her towards her dream, I was secretly trying to sabotage her. I was secretly hoping she would fail. That was *just one* of many unspoken thoughts I harbored. Not surprisingly, with unconscious thoughts like that, the marriage did not survive.

## Sharing Secrets Safely

A very powerful exercise that we learned in our training which Stav and I continue to practice and teach others is how to share secrets safely. Whenever we are about to embark on a new venture or just need to share, we sit facing each other, we remember to breathe, and Person A shares their secrets thoughts (in short sentences) while the other (Person B) merely responds with "Thank you." Person A should not try to explain or defend whatever they are sharing. The purpose of this exercise is to just expose and release secret fears. For example:

Person A: *"A secret fear I have around you starting this new job is that you won't have time for me."*

Person B: *"Thank you"* (Remember to breathe and be defenseless.)

Person A: *"A secret thought I have around you starting this new job is that I hope you fail."*

Person B: *"Thank you"*

Person A: *"A secret fear I have around you starting this new job is that you'll meet somebody new and leave me."*

Person B: *"Thank you"*

Continue in this manner until Person A no longer has any secret thoughts or fears to share. Then switch and now Person B says his/her secret thoughts and fears with Person A responding with "Thank you."

Very often you will find that both of you have the same thoughts and fears. Now, instead of feeling guilty and isolated for whatever fears you have, you can both now acknowledge that you are the same.

Finally, redo the process again, but this time, instead of sharing your secret thoughts and fears, share your hopes, dreams and wishes.

Person A: *"The best thing that could happen around you starting this new job is that you'll make more money than you ever made and we'll always have enough.*

Person B: *"Thank you"*

Person A: *"The best thing that could happen around you starting this new job is that you'll feel better about yourself.*

Person B: *"Thank you"*

Person A: *"The best thing that could happen around you starting this new job is that we'll be able to buy a house.*

Person B: *"Thank you"*

This second part now cements the two of you into why you are embarking on this venture in the first place. It strengthens the love and hope between both of you.

Stav and I have learned to share all of our secret thoughts on any subject. We have seen the toll not sharing takes on people's lives, and do not want to pay it. When I wrote my first book, Stav shared all of her secret fears. She shared how there was a part of her that wanted me to fail. She shared how she was afraid that I would become famous and leave her. She shared how she was afraid that she would never be able to write her own book. I already knew her secret fears, because—I had the very same secret fears! I also feel those same fears when she goes for her dreams. In sharing our secret fears, we got to see that we are not bad for having those thoughts. Sharing our secret thoughts and fears increases our bonding and connection with one another. The more we practice this, the greater our intimacy. The greater our intimacy, the more solid our relationship becomes.

There is a sense of freedom we receive when we let go of our secret thoughts. We finally begin to see that inside ourselves we are many people—Gandhi, Mother Theresa, Hitler, Jesus, Stalin, etc. As we make peace with these people, we see that we are not bad for having secret, hateful thoughts—we are just afraid. The way out of the fear is shining the light of our love into the darkness.

# Self Discovery Quiz

- *If you had no secrets, how would you feel?*

- *What is a secret that you feel is really unforgivable? Is God big enough to forgive it? Are you big enough to forgive it?*

- *Imagine a secret that you feel is really horrible. Now imagine a good friend telling you that they have that secret and how ashamed they are of it. What would you tell them?*

- *Are there any family secrets that everybody knows but nobody acknowledges? Is there a family member that nobody talks about? What do you want to do about it?*

- *Is there a subject that your family does not talk about? Why?*

- *Have you ever found it hard to keep a secret? Why?*

- *Do you have secrets that you are secretly proud of?*

- *What is your worst secret? How is your life affected by always trying to hide it?*

- *What is a secret you would like to release? Who would be a safe person to confess it to?*

*Until one is committed, there is hesitancy, the chance to draw back, always ineffectiveness. Concerning all acts of initiative, there is one elementary truth, the ignorance of which kills countless ideas and splendid plans: That the moment one definitely commits oneself, then Providence moves too. All sorts of things occur to help one that would otherwise never have occurred. A whole stream of events issues from the decision, raising in one's favor all manner of unforeseen incidents and meetings and material assistance, which no man could have dreamt would have come his way.*

*I have a deep respect for one of Goethe's couplets:*

> *"Whatever you can do,*
> *or dream you can—begin it.*
> *Boldness has genius, power,*
> *and magic in it."*

**W. N. Murray**

*You cannot be totally committed sometimes.*
**A Course in Miracles Text** pg. 117 / 127

# Commit or Get Off The Pot!

D o you want to get excited about life once
again?

Do you want to see your life change in ways
you never thought possible?

Do you want to move those mountains of despair from
your past?

Then begin to commit in all aspects of your life.

The word *commitment* scares the hell (or rather, heaven)
out of many people. To the world it means *until death do us part—*
forever. It generally conjures up images in people of being trapped,
feeling controlled and being stuck forever.

The ego loves concepts like this because then it can use fear
to manipulate us from ever taking *any step* towards our dreams. A
relationship based on the concept of "until death do us part" is prac-
tically impossible. You can almost hear the death knell of the
relationship. How many couples have you seen that are committed
"until death do us part" and yet the relationship is dead? Only a shell
exists, but any true feelings are long gone.

The fear of committing *forever* scares many people away from
even starting to open up to another person. This fear not only pertains to relationships but also to our dreams. We are so afraid of
making a mistake and looking stupid that we avoid any commitment at all to keep us safe. And yet, deep inside, we feel unsettled
and restless because we know we should be taking our steps.

A committed relationship is not based on whether you stay
together until "death do us part." An intimate, committed relationship is one which implies *sexual exclusivity* in which both partners

agree that **for as long as they are committed to each other**, they will behave in a way that does not violate each other's trust. It is a commitment to both partners growing and learning about themselves. It is the feeling that we are committed to each other's growth, **right now** regardless of how the relationship ends. True commitment has nothing to do with bodies occupying the same proximity and neither is it based on a marriage license. True commitment starts in the heart and then moves outward.

Now, I am not saying that I am opposed to people committing to one another for the rest of their lives, but how many of us know our partners deeply enough when we marry to intelligently make that decision? How many of us know the future and everything that will happen? For that matter, how many of us know **ourselves** deeply enough? How many of us get into abusive relationships and then feel trapped by the words "until death do us part?"

Commitment, as the world views it, says that we will stay together for the rest of our lives and **never change**. Who we are today is who we will be 40 years from now. How safe! How boring!

I believe that commitment is a moment by moment choice and that many of us have a hard time even being committed for the moment. How many times have you been on a date, and all the while you're looking at other men or women? Or you may even be thinking about the person you're going to see the following evening. You are not even committed in the moment to the person you are with!

And yet, for all the problems that commitment offers, no true relationship will ever last **unless both parties are committed**. When times get rocky in a marriage, it is only the commitment of the partners that can see the marriage past the stormy points.

Stav and I are committed to each other for the rest of our lives, but we also know that this world is a world of change. We know that our marriage can change at any time. We can get sick and die or circumstances can separate us. One of us may suddenly realize that their dream is to move to India and feed the hungry. But that doesn't stop us from committing to each other. Once again, *com-*

*mitment has **nothing** to do with bodies living in the same house.* It is a bonding of our hearts and souls to each other's hopes and dreams and supporting those dreams whether we physically are together or not. It is a commitment to the highest aspects of our Self and it is a commitment to supporting our partner's highest aspects of their Self. We hope and pray that our relationship is a long and happy one—together, but we also know sometimes our Higher Self has other plans.

So, we commit to each other moment by moment. We commit to treat each other with respect, dignity, love and affection, moment by moment. And in that moment, I allow myself to feel that this relationship is "until death do us part."

A saying that Stav and I particularly like is, "You can never be committed to the wrong thing." What this means is that, as soon as you commit to a course of action, feelings will begin to surface. You will experience fear and excitement, uncertainty and faith—and all the while, the Universe will begin to show you whether this decision is the correct one. If you commit to opening that restaurant you always wanted to open, but the loans fall through, you can't get the building permits and nothing seems to work, this may be an indication that this is not the right time to proceed. Or conversely, everything seems to go smoothly, deadlines are handled, leases are signed and differences are ironed out. But either way, you will have an indication if this is the time to open the restaurant. By not committing (or acting) at all, you never find out.

There is an episode on an old TV show that demonstrated the power of making a commitment. Howard, the accountant for a small town, decides one day to quit his job and become a beachcomber.

"I'm going to live off the fat of the land and take it easy! I'm finally going to be my own boss."

The guys at the barbershop give him a hard time. But he quits his job anyway and moves down to the beach.

After about two weeks, though, Howard begins to get bored. He starts missing his old job and old friends. So, after a few more days, he returns to his town and gets his old job back. Later, in the barbershop, the other guys are razzing him for quitting his job to be a beachcomber and then coming back. But the sheriff says,

"Well, at least now he *knows* he doesn't want to be a beachcomber."

By committing, Howard learned something about himself. He learned that he needed time for himself and also that he didn't want to be a beachcomber. Now, he could release that dream and start working on the next.

You are the only one who can decide the level of commitment that you want. Never let the world dictate terms that you are not comfortable with. When working on your relationship, committing to each other is the opportunity for both of you to grow, to learn how to express your truth, how to negotiate and how to listen. The reason one commits is because there is an immense payoff in trusting that God will help you and that you also have the power to do it. **Commitment harnesses the *intellectual* power of our minds with the *faith* of our hearts, and together this power can, literally, move mountains.**

Committing to the growth and well-being of each person takes discipline and courage. It is giving your heart fully to a person or a dream, knowing that there are no guarantees. It's trusting the Divine spirit within you to guide and help you each step of the way, because the only way to live life, in my opinion, is to live with commitment, with excitement, with vigor. A relationship is not how long we stay together, but what we learn and enjoy **while** we are together. When you commit, the only person that you are truly committing to is **yourself**. Commitment brings up all those feelings of "What if?" and "Am I good enough?" and "Is he/she good enough?" By committing while experiencing those feelings we learn that we are "good enough" and that we can handle the "what ifs."

Remember that commitment is a moment by moment choice. *A Course in Miracles* says that every thought we have takes us her closer to love or closer to fear. Commitment is the same way.

Every thought or action brings us either closer together or further apart. When you commit to not use foul language when arguing, you will be tempted, very tempted, to do so anyway. But ask yourself, in that moment: does this act take me closer or farther away from love? Will this word or action enhance our relationship or knock off a chip from our foundation? Though in the moment it may seem easier to fall back on old modes of operating, committing to a new, healthier path allows everybody to grow.

Another reason I find commitment essential is that it helps a couple outlast the normal cycles and changes that occur in every relationship. You know the changes I'm talking about. Like the day you suddenly realize that you're not having sex as often as you used to. That the sexual passion has died and that you feel more like brother and sister than lovers. I've seen relationships die at this point, because people think that that is what a relationship is about—hearts pounding in lust, sweating bodies, love notes and flirtations. When it changes, it *seems* that the love has gone.

The love has not gone. However, now we get to face the real growth in a relationship—the day-to-day challenges of just loving ourselves and each other. When Stav and I hit this point, initially we became afraid and thought that the physical love had gone. Fortunately, we had enough experience to also know that this feeling was temporary and that our relationship was actually rising to a higher level. We stuck to our commitment to each other, shared our fears, communicated more and looked inside our hearts. And the passion came back. What actually happened was that we were letting other activities and priorities take precedence. *We were not connected.* By staying committed, looking at our issues and reconnecting, the passion returned.

We now know that we go through cycles in our relationship. There are times when we feel very passionate for each other. Other times we feel like brother and sister. There are times when we enjoy each other's company and times when just seeing the other person makes us feel irritated. A well-known adage in the stock market is that if you want to consistently make money, you have to invest for the long term. The losers in the market are those who sell when times get tough, when it looks as if the stocks are not doing well. But over time, the market always recovers, and those who stick with it recover also.

It is important to remember that no thought or feeling is permanent, that we all go through sane cycles and crazy cycles, generous cycles and stingy cycles, open cycles and closed cycles, winter and summer. It is the power of your commitment that will help you survive the winter of your discontent in order to harvest the rewards of your summer of growth.

An example of a personal commitment I have is that every morning, no matter what, I give my wife a kiss before I go to work. Every morning. No matter what. That means that I give her a kiss whether I am mad at her or not, whether we are happy with each other or fighting. If I am angry with her, it may be just a quick, cold peck on the cheek before I hurry out, but I kiss her anyway. Why? Because I have learned that the most precious thing in this world is the love we have for each other. The most important thing in our relationship is not about who is right or wrong, but about getting back to the love that we *know* we have for each other—even when we are angry.

Kissing Stav, even when I am angry, always softens my heart, whether I want it to or not. While I am taking my morning shower and I am busy hating her, I know that I am going to *have* to kiss her before I leave. I dread it! I hate it! My ego feels insulted and tries to convince me, just this once, *"don't do it."* But my deepest truth is that truly, I love her and I will keep my personal commitment.

After I kiss her, I may still be angry, but it's hard to stay that way. Invariably, by around 10 o'clock, I feel like I miss her and I call her (or she calls me) just to connect. We may still have a ways to go toward resolving our differences, but now we are back on the path.

Let go of your thoughts that commitment means *forever*. If the thought of living with someone for the rest of your life is too scary, pick a length of time that feels just scary enough, but short enough that you can stick it out. When Stav and I first got into a committed relationship, we were scared, fearful but wanting to open up to love. So what we did was to commit to each other for six months. No matter what happened, we would not end the relationship for any reason until the six-month period was up. At the end of that period, we could decide to do another six months or end our relationship.

There was no guarantee that the relationship would last, but we were committed to sticking it out for the agreed upon time period because we *knew* that there would be good times and there would be hard times. We *knew* that our issues were going to come up and, instead of running away from them like we did in past relationships, we wanted to try something new. We also *knew* that our partner could indeed help us to be a better person.

We actually wrote a contract specifying the length of time for the commitment, and stating that we were not allowed to date anyone else during that time. We also listed all of the conditions we wanted to be honored during the term of the contract. Conditions such as:

*"We will not leave the room when we are arguing."*

*"We will spend quality time each week together. For now, every Friday night."*

*"We must both agree before committing to any major financial purchases."*

*"We will not call each other names or abuse each other in any way when we are angry."*

This may seem like a silly exercise, but believe me, just sitting down with your partner and developing agreements to live by is a big commitment in itself.

Both of us let ourselves feel all the things that went wrong in our past relationships, and we used them to change our current relationship. Committing for six months gave us both the secure feeling that no matter what, we would stay together. It also gave us the escape valve that if the relationship *was* horrible, well, after six months it was over. It also gave both of us a feeling of safety and relief to know what was expected and how we wanted to be treated.

Did we honor all of the terms in the contract all of the time? Of course not! The truth is, when we get into our egos, we **want** to break all the rules and flaunt our authority. We want to hurt the other person and rub their nose in the fact that we can defy their *petty* rules. But you know, I found that by at least committing to that piece of paper, there were times when I stopped following my ego and remembered our original agreements and why we made them in the first place. They were developed to help us to succeed as a couple. I realized that even if I followed the agreements one out of ten times, I was 10% saner. And the more I committed to keeping my word, the more trustworthy I showed myself, and the more peaceful our life became. Now, committing to a sane mind is what Stav and I try to affirm and teach all the time.

As I said earlier, developing this contract is an act of commitment in itself. It will bring up lots of feelings in both of you, so don't be surprised if there is resistance in doing it.

I was working with a couple whose six-month marriage was already chaotic with unexpressed expectations, misunderstandings and disappointments. I suggested that they start their marriage over and write a contract clearly spelling out each of their needs and expectations. I made it clear that they **both** had to be in agreement on any issue before it could be entered into the contract. Initially the wife seemed excited about this idea but the husband was subdued and quiet. I sent them away, to return the following week with a draft of their ideas.

The next week they returned with just a few thoughts that the husband had written, but neither had really sat down to address the issue. So I decided to have them do the process in my office. It was surprising to see the switch in feelings. Whereas the wife was initially excited over the idea, now she suddenly seemed to withdraw. Her husband, on the other hand, wholeheartedly got into the process, scribbling his ideas and prompting her for her suggestions. Something was wrong here, so I asked her,

"Jana, you suddenly seem to me as if you don't want to do this process. What's going on?"

"Oh, I don't know. I just don't have any ideas right now."

"Correct me if I'm wrong, but it seems to me as if there is more going on. Why don't you take a deep breath and tell me how you are really feeling right now?"

She took a deep breath, looked at me and replied, "You know, doing this contract does not seem romantic at all! It's like we're writing a business proposal!"

I laughed. "Of course it does! Do you realize that we spend more time and preparation opening a business, but never do the same in opening our hearts? If we opened a business the same way we start a relationship, it would look something like this:

'Uh, Sir, I would like to apply to your bank for a $100,000 loan. I don't know what I will do with the money or how it will be spent, but I am really trustworthy and promise to pay you back—really I will.'"

She smiled at my illustration.

"I know it doesn't feel romantic," I continued, "but in the long run, you'll both benefit."

And so she began to get into the spirit of the process.

The following week there was a dramatic change in their attitude.

"This contract idea has been great," she started out. "I know at first I resisted, but now I feel that we both know what we expect from each other. I've been able to express my fears and doubts and he's been able to express his. It feels like we're finally talking."

"And you know what else?" she added. "I find myself not having angry conversations in my head at him throughout the day because of what *I think* he may not be doing. Now we have agreements and I am finding out that he does follow through on his part. Now I return home from work not as irritated as I used to."

Following this chapter is a Relationship Contract that Stav and I use in our workshops. Use it and alter it in any way you see fit. Make it work for you. And remember, forgive yourself when you slip up. Commitment is about freedom—the freedom to be, express, and live the Divine person you truly are. Commit to that and you, your relationships, and the world will rejoice.

# Affirmations

- *The only person I truly need to commit to is myself.*
- *God has never let me down. Even in my darkest hour He was there.*
- *I can never commit to the wrong thing.*
- *When I commit, the world always lets me know whether my decision is right or wrong. Then I can choose again.*
- *I now commit to my life. I cannot lose.*
- *I now commit to seeing the love that has always existed in my relationships.*
- *As I commit more to love, fear loses its ability to frighten me.*
- *I now expect and receive the best from others.*
- *Nobody loses when I commit.*
- *In commitment is my freedom.*

# Relationship Contract

This contract is between _( name )_ and _( name )_ and is to be in effect from _( date )_ to _( date )_. Because we love and trust each other, under **no circumstances** will we end this relationship during this period. At the end of this period we can choose to continue our relationship or not. Any other changes to this contract must be agreed upon by **both** of us.

The Purpose of our relationship is: _____
(Ex: To heal, have fun, grow. To learn to trust each other, etc.)

In order to enhance the love, trust and respect we claim for each other, we now agree to the following conditions: *(Add or delete any conditions you desire here)*

I agree to always tell my truth, to the best of my ability.

I agree that I am not responsible for your feelings and you are not responsible for mine. I will honor and respect your feelings, even if I do not agree with them.

I will ask you for what I want. I will not make it necessary to play guessing games. I will be as clear as possible with my desires.

I agree that I am not responsible for your sexuality and you are not responsible for mine.

Financial agreements: _____
(Ex: You pay all the bills while I go to school, then we switch. I pay the rent and utilities, you pay for groceries and entertainment. We will not make major purchases without checking it out with our partner, etc. . . .)

When we are angry with each other:_____

(Ex: We will not use foul language or hit one another. We can call someone for support. We will not leave the room. We will scream into a pillow, or hit the bed with a tennis racket in order to release anger and tension and then proceed. . . .)

Play agreements: _____

(Ex: Once a week we will go out together for time alone. It's OK to go out with your friends and I can go out with mine. On Tuesdays we schedule nothing, just time to relate, have sex, enjoy ourselves.)

Name _____      Name_____

Date _____

*You can add anything you want into this contract, as long as both of you agree. So allow your wishes, fears and anything else to come up so they can be addressed. You can also renegotiate any agreement that is not working out for either one or both of you. Remember that both of you are human beings, not robots. At times you may break a condition on this contract, either through forgetfulness or just plain old brattiness. At that point you need to ask your partner for forgiveness. Forgive yourself. Forgive your partner. Make forgiveness a daily act. The whole point of being in a relationship is to expand the love you have for yourself and others. And to have fun. Don't lose track of that point.*

# Love Yourselves, No Matter What!

*Don't carry a grudge.*
*While you're carrying the grudge*
*the other guy's out dancing.*

**Buddy Hackett**


*Resentment is like taking poison and waiting for*
*the other person to die.*

**Malachy McCourt**


*You cannot get ahead*
*if you spend all your time getting even.*

**Rep. Dick Armey**


*No matter how difficult the past,*
*you can always begin again today.*

**Buddha**

**One Big Happy**

© By permission of Rick Detorie and Creators Syndicate

# Release the Past

Creating a relationship that feeds your soul requires that ultimately, you revisit your past, process the feelings around it, embrace it and then release it. *A Course in Miracles* states, *"The past is over. It can touch me not."* WB Lesson # 289

Everything that has been discussed in the previous chapters ultimately hinges on releasing our past, or in other words, forgiveness. When we are in a state of unforgiveness, it taints and ruins every aspect of our lives. Unforgiveness is why many of us walk around feeling hostile, cynical and bitter. Unforgiveness is why we hold onto secrets, why we have low self-esteem, why we defend ourselves. Unforgiveness is what keeps us repeating the same mistake over and over. Unforgiveness keeps us in reactivity. Unforgiveness is what erects barriers to love, instead of developing healthy boundaries. And unforgiveness robs us of our lives in the present. We spend our lives reliving old hurts or reacting to a *perceived* threat based on an old hurt, and in the process, we let precious moments of love slip through our fingers.

The movie *Dead Man Walking* is a powerful story of love and forgiveness. In it, Sister Mary Prejean has been asked to be the spiritual counselor to Matthew Poncelet, who is scheduled to be executed by lethal injection for the rape and murder of a young couple. The movie is a pilgrimage for both the nun and the convict. Sister Prejean gets to see her own judgments and fears, and in the process makes many mistakes and wonders whether she is just wasting her time with this *lost cause.*

She meets with the parents of the murdered boy and girl, with differing results. The parents, understandably, want Matthew executed. But, the father of the murdered boy, though he is full of hate and rage, begins his own process of healing after his wife leaves him. He goes to group sessions with other parents of children who have been killed. He begins the process of not only feeling the hate and rage, but also sadness and compassion for others.

At Matthew's funeral, after his execution, Sister Prejean sees the father of the boy that Matthew murdered standing at the edge of the cemetery. She approaches him and thanks him for coming.

"I don't know why I came, Sister. I have so much hate and anger in me. I wish I had your faith."

"It's not faith," she replies. "It's work."

The closing scene of the movie shows the grieving father and the nun, praying in church, doing the work.

In this movie I found it sad that it wasn't until the last twenty minutes of his life that Matthew Poncelot could drop his defenses enough to see that he was loved and also to own up to his part in the murders. It took him a whole lifetime to finally come to a place where he had nowhere else to go but to surrender to the possibility that he was responsible for what he did *and* that he was **b** a child of God.

How long do you want to take before you let God's love in? How long do you want to take before you begin to see *your part* in every relationship you ever had? How long do you want to take before you forgive everyone who hurt you in the past, so that you can now start living the life you want to live?

These are not easy questions, but they must be asked. Forgiveness is not a *thing you do* but a *process you experience*. It is not a mental act but a heartfelt movement. I have seen people try to practice forgiveness by basically imitating the Cowardly Lion in *The Wizard of Oz.*

"I do forgive. I do forgive. I do! I do! I do! I do forgive!"

They say it over and over, like a mantra, like a magic charm, thinking that that is forgiveness. As a spiritual counselor, I have seen many people *insist* that they have forgiven their parents or an ex-lover, while their faces flush with unexpressed anger, their fingers jiggle and their eyes twitch. They tap their feet in irritation as I pursue anything that deals with the "forgiven" person. Sometimes, I actually lose a client, so afraid are they to see what is *really* going on. I actually had a client once tell me regarding her ex-husband, "I forgave the jerk years ago!" never realizing the extent of rage she still harbored toward him.

Something I want to stress here is, do not! Do Not! **Do Not! DO NOT**! forgive anybody, until you see there is a *personal benefit for you* in forgiving. The act of forgiveness is not about letting somebody off the hook, it's not about pretending that what happened to us did not really affect us, it's not about turning a blind eye from our past. True forgiveness repairs our present life because we are releasing thoughts that are hurting our present life. For many of us it may take time before we can see how holding onto unforgiven incidents are impacting and sabotaging *our* lives.

Forgiveness is a process that starts in the head (intellect), travels through our heart (feelings) and ends in our soul. We may initially be introduced to the idea of forgiveness because it is the right thing to do, or because Jesus would do it. But, for many of us, there is pain and hurt around the issue. And pain and hurt can only be addressed in the heart—not the head.

As I began to see how my thoughts created my reality, I began to see the part I played in my upbringing, how both my mom and I were playing out our individual scripts. And so, as I started to see my part, I began to "forgive" my mom for not knowing any better. (How superior!) I began to rationalize that "she did the best she could. She just didn't know any better."

Luckily, I had a teacher, who would constantly remind me,

"So, I'm glad you *forgive* your mom for not knowing any better. But Jerry ... how ... do ... you ... feel? How do you *feel* about how you were raised?"

I had now entered a paradoxical part of my spiritual progress. Whenever I thought that I had forgiven my mom, Joe would remind me to check in on how I felt. Every time I checked in with my heart, I found I still felt angry and resentful. I still felt that she was wrong and had hurt me. You see, Joe was doing me a great favor. He was teaching me that forgiveness takes not only the willingness to change my mind, but also the work to change my heart. No matter what my mind would say, ("Forgive. It's good to forgive. God forgives, so should you,") my heart would still tell me how I *truly felt* emotionally. This was a time when I was using Breath Integration intensely to allow myself to feel and release all my stored up hate and rage.

Then one day, after months of allowing myself to just feel angry about how I was raised, a wonderful thing happened. I checked in my heart, and the hate and rage were smaller. I actually felt some real love for my mother. There was still anger, but I also saw an end to it. I was reaching a point where my **thoughts** of forgiveness were beginning to match my **feelings** of forgiveness. This did not last, of course. I still had a way to go. The difference was that I now *knew* that there was an end to the hate and the pain. Over the next few months I seemed to take giant steps in healing my relationship with my mother. Additionally, my relationships with women began to change for the better.

Forgiveness is a very selfish act because the person who benefits the most is the person doing the forgiving. Unforgiveness keeps us in a state of hell, fear and stress—while the *perpetrator* goes on with their life, probably unaware of our hurt and anger. All the while that I was processing my rage and hurt toward my mom, do you know what she was doing? She was living in Hawaii! Enjoying life! While I suffered!

Even if you are not ready to forgive, I want you to see the cost you pay for holding onto your grudges. Whenever somebody does us harm and we hold onto the harm, we are making a decision about the world and then applying it in our lives. For example, think of an incident in which you were hurt. Now list all the decisions you made around the incident. For example, let's say you were hurt in a relationship because your partner left you for another. You may have made decisions like:

"Women/men can't be trusted."

"Other people are always trying to take away what I love."

"You can't trust anyone."

"Love isn't safe."

These are just a few of the thoughts and decisions we may create. These decisions then become laws within our mind and we begin to act as if they are true. We see *all* women as untrustworthy. We feel paranoid because others *always* want to take away our good. We can't trust and be open to receiving love without thinking that there is some cost. Remember that all of our thoughts create, and the thoughts we think, whether conscious or unconscious, continue to manifest. With thoughts like these, how successful do you think you will be in creating a wonderful, conscious relationship with another person? Those negative decisions that we treasure keep us from getting the relationship that we desire. They are the blocks to our happiness.

Forgiveness is the process of slowly releasing those laws in our minds. It may start by changing the thought, "Women can't be trusted" into "*Some* women can't be trusted, but there are many more who can." This statement supports the belief that it is *still possible* to have a real relationship with another. As you forgive more and more, you may refine that decision into, "Women can be trusted, because *I* can be trusted. I now take responsibility for *my* part in every relationship."

So, if you are willing, practice this exercise in *any part* of your life that isn't working. If your prosperity is lacking, list who hurt you around money and then list the decisions you made around money and prosperity. If your sex life isn't happy, list those who hurt you regarding sex, and list the decisions you made around your sexuality. If your career isn't fulfilling, list who taught you that life was hard and unrewarding, and list the decisions you made around working for a living. Then look at all those decisions, and begin to write new decisions that support where you want to go instead of where you currently are. Ultimately, you will get to the point of forgiving yourself for making these decisions in the first place. Now, that is progress!

Unforgiveness keeps our hearts in prison.

*A Course in Miracles* says,

> *Who could be set free while he imprisons anyone? A jailer is not free, for he is bound together with his prisoner. He must be sure that he does not escape, and so he spends his time in keeping watch on him. The bars that limit him become the world in which his jailer lives, along with him. And it is on his freedom that the way to liberty depends for both of them.*
>
> *Therefore, hold no one prisoner. Release instead of bind, for thus are you made free.*

**Workbook pg. 356 / 366**

When Stav and I are working with someone who needs to release the past, the question we always ask is whether the person is *willing* to forgive the perpetrator, even if he/she doesn't **actually forgive** the person for a hundred years, or a hundred lifetimes. We don't ask them to forgive the person, just to be *willing* to forgive. You need to remember that our true identity is with spirit, and to our spirits, time is an illusion. As soon as the person says that they would be *willing* to forgive at some unspecified time, you can almost see their spirits sigh with relief! Because the spirit now knows that whether it takes two minutes or two hundred years, there will be an end to the pain and someday love will once again be shared.

How can you tell whether forgiveness is needed in your life? Well, Edwine Gaines, a powerful prosperity teacher, has a little exercise that helps people to determine whether forgiveness is needed in their lives. What she does is to have them stand up, look down at their bodies and ask the question, "Am I in a body?" If the answer is "yes," then forgiveness is needed. As long as we live in our limited bodies, with our limited perceptions, we will be tempted to see things in our own limited way. We will perceive hurt where there was none and pain where there was a lesson. Forgiveness is the opportunity to see the world with new eyes, to change our perceptions, to create miracles.

Do not be afraid to ask for help when dealing with forgiveness issues. Many of us have been abused, beaten, reviled, insulted and hurt. Forgiveness is not to be taken lightly. It is not a one-day workshop and then you're done. When you decide to work on forgiveness, know that it will take time—months, years, maybe even decades. But, know this. **There is an end to the pain!** So, hire a therapist, minister or coach. Get into groups where people are truly working on their issues and aren't afraid to help you work on yours. As you build the peace in your heart, stone by stone, you will find that you are building an altar for peace, an altar to love and lightheartedness.

# The Stages of Forgiveness

Stav and I have been teaching workshops on forgiveness for many years. In our own personal process of forgiveness, and in the Forgiveness Workshops we teach, we have found that the steps to forgiving mirror the steps of Elisabeth Kubler-Ross's model of grief. We have also added some of our own steps here.

At some point or other, we need to experience each of these steps to fully heal. We cannot skip these steps. We will not necessarily follow these steps in order, and we may even repeat steps, but each step will, at some point, be taken. Stav and I have seen people stuck for years in sadness over an incident, but they never let themselves feel the anger. Or they get stuck in anger, never letting their defenses down to let their hearts soften enough to feel the sadness and hurt. And so, true healing is delayed until the person allows every step to be experienced.

# Shock

Any time we experience a loss or offense, we first go into shock. This is a self-protective mechanism that buys us time. Shock is a totally natural process that numbs out our feelings and allows us to continue (for awhile) whatever needs to be done. For example, shock allows us to rescue a child from a burning building, or to carry a fellow wounded soldier to safety without having to process the feelings involved. It is not uncommon that after a heroic act, the hero (or heroine) can be seen getting dizzy and even vomiting, as the full impact hits them. Shock gives us time to acclimate to what has happened and come to grips with the issue.

But experiencing lots of hurts and losses keeps us in a state of chronic shock that ultimately leads to a state of chronic numbness. We feel cut off from our feelings. People with many childhood wounds can live in a perpetual state of shock. To start the forgiveness process, you must be able to learn to identify your feelings. People who are in shock generally do not know what their feelings are.

Most of our work with a new client usually involves teaching the person about feelings. It is amazing how many people live in a state of "no pain." There is no joy, no love, no fear—no pain. Nothing. The deeper the injury, the longer it may take for the person to begin to feel anything.

# Denial

After the shock wears off, people generally negate the reality of the offense or loss and try to move on with their life. This would work if we *really believed* that we were not hurt, but we don't. Ignoring the hurt and the wound only creates bigger problems later in life. We find ourselves living lives *at the effect* of what happened to us, and never being fully alive. We can stay stuck in this stage because it seems less painful to live a lie instead of facing the truth. Much of the work done in therapy/healing groups revolves around acknowledging the wounds we received, sharing it with others and then facing the sadness and disappointment of our childhood. Another way we may deny what happened is by minimizing it. We may tell ourselves, "It wasn't that bad, it's not a big deal. Daddy's really too busy for me, it's OK. At least, he's not as bad as Tommy's dad."

For a long time, I couldn't accept getting angry with my parents because, after all, "My parents weren't alcoholics, so what do I have to complain about?" The denial of my own basic pain, though, kept showing up in my relationships. I kept creating people in my life who triggered the buttons that reminded me of my issues with my folks. No amount of telling people that I had a good childhood could convince my heart that the pain did not matter. For years I was just fooling myself.

# Bargaining

We may also try bargaining the offense by explaining it away. It is always a way of postponing looking at the issues at hand. We postpone looking at our real feelings of anger, hurt and rage with statements like: "Maybe he didn't mean it," or "She did the best she could." Or, we postpone by doubting our own perceptions. "Maybe I imagined it. Maybe I'm just exaggerating." Or even, "I deserved it."

Another way of bargaining is where we actually try to make up with the perpetrator in an effort to get them to stop the way they have been acting. We hope to get on their good side, and maybe, because we are so good, they will stop treating us so badly.

The sad part is that the people who bargain tend to minimize everything in their life—the good and the bad.

# Anger

The first three stages can be considered as the pre-forgiveness stages.

Now we are on the threshold of *possible* healing. When we can fully *feel* the immensity of the loss or offense, then we are on our way to forgiveness—unless we choose to stay stuck in resentment. Anger needs to be expressed safely and responsibly. I have worked with many people who just sit and stew in their anger and resentment. They are victims and stay there. Others may become rage-aholics—going through life raging and making everybody pay for somebody else's mistake. Being in a state of unforgiveness keeps us from releasing the emotional toxins that build up over time. Feeling our anger is a step toward draining away the poisons in our life and having cleaner, healthier relationships

Anger is not about getting someone to pay for what they did or trying to get the world to make it up to us. That only leads to years of disappointment. Healthy anger is the feeling we get when we tell ourselves the **truth** about the impact of the offense. When we finally allow ourselves to feel, "Never again will I allow this to happen to me!" then healthy anger can lead to positive change. Healthy anger can lead to reforms in government and the crackdown on abuse. Healthy anger led Gandhi to defy the British government with nonviolent resistance. He saw what was wrong and changed it. He didn't use anger to destroy. He used it to free a country.

Many of us are afraid of our anger. Many of us have a belief that anger is bad and that, "If I let my anger out, it will hurt somebody." Many of us have experienced destructive, toxic anger and have confused the angry actions with the feeling of anger. We inadvertently associate *feeling* angry with *acting* angry and think that if we feel angry, we have to act it out.

Anger is an emotion—just like our other emotions. The problem is that you cannot suppress one emotion without suppressing all the rest. Or we may suppress our anger by feeling another, safer emotion, such as sadness (see the next section.) Suppressing your anger may make you feel better—for awhile—but it also suppresses your sadness, your grief, your joy, your happiness and your aliveness. And not surprisingly, since they are getting no emotional energy, your dreams die as well.

Once again, if you are new to anger or are afraid of it, get a therapist who works with this powerful feeling. The question you should ask yourself whenever you are feeling angry is, "What is my intention in expressing this feeling?" If your intention is to punish or make another person wrong, your anger will come out as attack. If your intention is to heal and validate yourself, to honor your feelings of anger so that you can free yourself from the past, it will be constructive.

There were times that my anger *felt* destructive, as I raged over my past with my counselor and classmates. However, even though it *felt* destructive, it was actually constructive because I was learning to vent and express my frustration in *appropriate* ways. I had teachers and classmates who guided me through my rage. I was taught how to feel and express the anger without projecting it outward, thereby creating more pain, guilt and attack. I was taught how to take responsibility for my own rage without blaming everybody else. As I began to allow my anger to be expressed, it felt as if a dam had burst. I was more open to feeling not only my anger, but also my hurt, my pain and finally, my joy.

One word of caution: It is **not** a good idea to call your parents and dump on them. Raging at them only creates more discord and pain and keeps the negative cycles in place. They do not need your anger. **You** are the one that is healing—not them. There may be a time, after a long period of healing, that you may be able to talk to them, if the door is open, but only after **you** have handled your issues.

So, instead of running from your anger, learn how to use it. In our work we use techniques such as screaming into a pillow, hitting a heavy bag with a baseball bat, or hitting a bed with a tennis racket to churn up and release anger. One technique I find especially helpful when expressing anger is to imagine seeing the person you are angry at, and tell them,

"The purpose of expressing and releasing my rage at you is so that someday I will actually forgive you. My purpose is for me to find peace."

Initially, most people stay stuck in one of the above four stages, cycling from one to another. The next stages are the more feeling and progressively healing stages.

## Sadness

If you have been nurturing sadness over an incident for years, without any sense of release, I want you to know that that is not sadness. It is anger in the disguise of sadness. It's sitting in victimization and resentment.

When we feel *healthy sadness*, there is ultimately a sense of release. If you feel as if you have been feeling sad for a long time with no release, you may want to try feeling some anger around the issue. And, of course, once again, get counseling. Healthy sadness is the emotion that heals the pain. All of our losses have to be grieved. Deepok Chopra says that the act of crying is not only emotional, but it is also physically healing. Allowing ourselves to feel our sadness and cry, we actually give our bodies and endorphin bath. Endorphins are the hormones that give us a sense of relaxation and well-being. That is why after we have a good cry, we feel better and more relaxed. In turn, this feeling of well-being strengthens the immune system, leading to a healthier psyche and a healthier body.

Being sad is being vulnerable. In order to better release the sadness, it helps to share the sadness with others. John Bradshaw talks about the concept of having a "Fair Witness," a counselor or group who witnesses to your pain and validates your experience. It is not about sympathy or having a pity party or blame session. It is about somebody validating your feelings and experiences. It can be very healing to hear, "You have every right to feel this way, I understand. . . etc." This gives you an opportunity to see that you are not wrong or crazy for having the thoughts and feelings you have. That *anyone* would feel the same way.

One danger that I have seen is that sometimes even after a person has been listened to and validated, they stay stuck in the drama. They show up session after session, group after group with the same old story. There comes a point where the person has to actively start changing their life.

Caroline Myss, in her book *Anatomy of the Spirit*, relates how some Native American Indian tribes handled a person who would hang onto an injury. Basically any member was allowed three times to tell the elders and the tribe their story. They could relate who had hurt them, how they were hurt and how they suffered. The person was listened to and given support and empathy. But after the third time, if the complaining persisted, the tribe would tell the person, "Enough! We have heard you and supported you. Now it is time for you to heal!" and everyone would turn their backs to him. Nobody would listen or give any more energy to the person's problems. What this encouraged was not only a support system for solving problems, but also a kick in the butt to those who wanted to hold onto old grievances.

I don't want you to think that you only get three chances to process before you're expected to change, because everybody has their own time table. But if you find that you are getting bored with another person's story (or even your own), then maybe it's time to say "Enough!"

Expressing and releasing our sadness in the presence of another is a way of once again building a sense of trust. When we were small, it may not have been safe to be vulnerable with those who hurt us. But by trusting once again we can then grieve our lost childhood, the lost trust, our lost innocence, and our lost dreams, and then claim the love and support we needed then, so we can begin the healing process now.

The healing emotion of sadness then leads to:

# *Acceptance*

In this stage we finally validate the experiences of our lives as we actually lived them. We face the fact that, indeed, "such-and-such" happened, and that it **HURT!** We no longer deny, rationalize or look the other way. We no longer pretend we had a wonderful childhood, great parents, etc. We stop lying to ourselves and *we* validate the experiences of our life as *we* experienced them.

As we come to more and more acceptance, this is now the time where forgiveness processes are the most helpful. A few of the most powerful that I have found are:

- *Sandra Ray has a forgiveness diet in which you write 70 times a day for 7 days "I now forgive you, ( name )." Remember to include a week for yourself.*

- *Marianne Williamson suggests that every night for 30 days you light a candle and pray for the person who hurt you.*

- *My father's method was that as he shaved every morning, he would repeat over and over,* "I now love ( name )."

# Forgiveness

One day, we suddenly realize we no longer feel the tension and charge around the incident or person. It doesn't come as a bolt of lightning. Usually it comes very quietly. There is a gradual realization that you're not hurting so much. You're not obsessing over the incident anymore. You may still feel *some* anger and resentment, but the pain has lessened. As Stav likes to remind people, "True forgiveness actually sneaks up on you."

Forgiveness does not in any way justify or condone the hurtful actions of others. Nor does it mean that you have to seek out or speak out against those who caused you harm. You can choose to never see them or confront them. If you are forgiving others for hurting you, it's helpful to tell yourself, "Never will I *knowingly* allow this to happen again!" This allows you to take responsibility for any part you may have played, and also to affirm that you will never allow that situation to happen again. And if it begins to happen again, *this time* you **will** speak up.

Forgiveness is letting go of the pain, the resentment, the outrage that you have been carrying as a burden for all these years. You may actually begin to remember the good things this person did. As I forgave my mom, I remembered the wonderful meals she made, how she used to read to me, my sixteenth surprise birthday party she planned, how she taught me to waltz, how she taught me to listen to music and see images and stories.

As I forgave my Mom, I found that I was able to forgive my past relationships with women. I began to remember why I got into a relationship with them in the first place. I remembered the dates, the sunsets, the camping trips, and all the love we shared.

I also began to feel compassion for the people who hurt me. At times, I was able to see my similarities to them. Ultimately, I was able to feel compassion for the wounding that they must have experienced in order for them to act the way they did.

As *A Course in Miracles* states,

> *To forgive is merely to remember only the loving thoughts you gave in the past, and those that were given you. All the rest must be forgotten. Forgiveness is a <u>selective remembering</u>, based not on your selection.*
> (Author's underlining)               **Text pg. 329 / 354**

Recently I had another experience of what forgiveness feels like. I was interviewed on television for my first book, *Compassionate Living - Everyday Spirituality*. In preparing for the interview, I decided to reread my book. And there were things that I wrote about, in that first book, that I had *totally* forgotten—incidents with my mother. As I was reading, it would hit me,

"Oh yeah, she did do that. Oh yeah, she used to be like that. Oh yeah, I used to be like that."

It was like I was reading a book written by another person. When I think about the incidents, I remember them, but there is no longer any charge around what happened. There is no longer any pain, remorse or even regret. All I feel now for my mom is that I love her. Plain and simple. Not that she did the best she could, but that she was/is the best. Plain and simple. I love her.

## *Peace and Joy*

As we truly forgive, we begin to feel compassion and understanding and connection with our true self and others. We are able to transcend the pain and hurt, and truly see the wounding that the perpetrator might have experienced in order to inflict the mean-spirited acts that hurt us. We are even able to see our similarities to them.

*A Course in Miracles* talks a lot about the concept of Atonement. The Atonement, as defined by *A Course in Miracles,* is not about "atoning or paying for one's sins," but rather it is the moment in time when *all of us* once again become One with ourselves, each other and with God. I like to break down the word as "At – One –Ment," which means to become "at – one" with ourselves and others.

We have so many compartments in our minds about who we think we are. We are afraid to embrace the Hitler, the murderers and the thieves in our own minds. Not accepting and forgiving those negative aspects keeps us in fear and prevents us from also embracing the Mother Theresa, Jesus, Buddha and the Gandhi in our minds. When we begin to become "at – one" with ourselves, we reconcile those separate areas into one *whole* person—a person who can be loving and generous at times, and unloving and stingy at other times.

We feel more comfortable in our skin. Just like we used to feel when we were very little, before comments and criticisms robbed us of our self love and acceptance.

When we reach this point, we feel more connected with ourselves and others. We see others with more compassion and love, and life becomes easier. We feel more light-hearted. We smile and laugh more. We take ourselves less seriously.

We have transcended our pain.

## *Go to the Beach!*

After all this work, there will be a time to rest, to relax, to play and enjoy the fruits of your labor.

Is that it? Is that the end? Of course not! We all have many things to forgive and to be forgiven. But I have found that forgiveness in one area of my life makes it easier to forgive in another. As I heal my relationship with my father, I find my relationships with men in general getting better. I find that people in authority no longer trigger my competitive, rebellious nature.

Remember that forgiveness is a process; it is an act of letting go of what we thought hurt us, and reclaiming once again that we are truly the children of a loving and gentle God.

One of my favorite forgiveness movies is *Field of Dreams*. Ray Kinsella hears a voice in his cornfield that tells him, "If you build it, he will come." He realizes through a vision that he should build a baseball field in order for his hero, Shoeless Joe Jackson, to come back and play baseball. Ray follows the vision, builds a field and Shoeless Joe comes back from death, to once again play baseball, along with other players who loved the sport. Then, Ray gets other messages, "Ease his pain," and "Go the distance." In each step, Ray follows his heart and does what's required.

In the end, Shoeless Joe finally shows Ray what all the fuss was about. Ray gets to see his father, alive again, as the young man he never knew—living his lost dream by playing catcher for a baseball team. As Ray stares at his dad, he remembers all those cryptic instructions he had been given. "If you build it, **he** will come," "Ease **his** pain," "Go the distance."

Ray whispers to his father, "It was you!" thinking the messages were in reference to his dad.

Shoeless Joe turns to Ray and replies, "No, Ray. It was *you*."

When we carry grudges, we are the ones in pain, the ones so far from our true Self. Forgiveness is not for others. Forgiveness is for ourselves. As we ease our past pain, our present pain diminishes. We feel more and more peace. As we go the distance into our heart, we find our heaven. And as we build an altar of love and forgiveness, He (God) will come.

*A Course in Miracles* states,

*The holiest of all the spots on earth is where an ancient hatred has become a present love.*

Text pg. 522 / 5\

# Self Discovery Quiz

- *Have you ever done something that you consider unforgivable? What do you need to do to change that perception?*

- *Did you ever swear to never act like your parents and found yourself doing the same things they did? Why? Can you forgive them and yourself for not knowing any better?*

- *Does it really feel that good to hold onto past pain?*

- *Are you afraid that if you forgive, it means that you condone those actions? Can you be forgiving and still work against child abuse? Can you be forgiving and still work against drunk driving? Does holding onto the pain, anger and unforgiveness make your crusade any more virtuous?*

- *What do you think God considers unforgivable? Is there really anything that cannot be forgiven?*

- *Select an incident from your past that you feel you are willing to work on in order to achieve forgiveness. Remember all the things that happened to you regarding the incident? Remember how you were hurt? Now write a story about that incident, but through the eyes of the person who hurt you. Write it from their perspective. Don't worry about whether you know the real facts or not. Just make it up as you go along and see what you create. And see how you feel later.*

# Using All This Stuff

*Now comes the fun part! This is where everything you* think *you know and everything you* want *to learn comes up. How willing are you to see another person's side? How willing are you to really want to change? How willing are you to claim a truly fulfilling relationship? How willing are you to see your innocence* and *the innocence in another? How willing are you to have your soul fed? How willing are you to feed another soul? Can it be done? Only if you want it badly enough and are willing to walk the walk. Only if you're willing to be happy* no matter what. *Only if you're ready for miracles.*

*My most brilliant achievement was being able to persuade my wife to marry me.*

**Winston Churchill**

*The only place where success comes before work is in the dictionary.*

**Vidal Sassoon**

*Try praising your wife even if it does frighten her at first.*

**Billy Sunday**

*Affirmations without action leads to delusion.*

**Larry Di Angi**

*In Paris they simply stared when I spoke to them in French; I never did succeed in making those idiots understand their own language.*

**Mark Twain**

*The man who makes no mistakes does not usually make anything.*

**Bishop W. C. Magee**

# How Do You Get to Carnegie Hall? Practice! Practice! Practice!

I was working out at my health club one day when I spotted Ray, the manager who sold us our memberships. He was also working out. I walked up to him and we chatted awhile, in between sweats and grunts.

"You know, Jerry," he puffed at one point, "selling this stuff – (huff) – is a lot easier – (puff) – than doing it."

I cracked up.

"Tell me about it!" I said, laughing. "It's the same thing with my counseling practice. It's always easier telling other people what to do than to do it myself."

I've covered lots of nice concepts in this book. What relationships are for, the laws that govern them and some basic foundations—connection, trust, boundaries, commitment, forgiveness, blah, blah-blah, blah-blah. Lots of *stuff* to think about.

Yet all of these concepts don't mean a thing until you actually apply them. It's like having an award-winning recipe for cheesecake in your head. All your thinking and talking about it won't produce a thing. Not until you actually mix the ingredients and bake it will you ever see if this cake really is a winner.

At some point, we all need to take a step toward love. We all need to take action. It is not good enough to just read a book or take a workshop and say to yourself, "Cool! Surrender to my partner. What a neat concept! I think *someday* I'll do that."

The real growth comes in *taking a step*—**any step**. Even if you do it wrong, you will still learn from it. So, don't judge whether you do it right or wrong. In fact, for awhile you will do many things wrong. But *A Course in Miracles* says that the *Course* (and life) is actually very simple. If a particular action works, if it takes you closer to love, keep it. If it doesn't work, drop it. We're the ones who make life hard and complex.

Whether you like it or not, right now, *you know* whether your relationships are feeding your soul. You can act dumb and pretend you don't know, but deep down inside, you know. And, you also know what you need to do. There is a step that you need to take; most likely it is a scary step—otherwise you would have done it years ago. Commit today to taking *some* action in your life that will be self-affirming.

This can take the form of speaking up to your partner, seeking counseling, committing to treating your partner in a more caring manner or even leaving an abusive relationship. You will find very quickly that there are many people who have experienced the same situations and changed their lives. You will find that you are not alone.

An example of just taking any step is when I published my first book, *Compassionate Living - Everyday Spirituality*. I had **no** idea what to do after the book was published. My mind was flooded with tons of questions,

"What will I do with all these books?"

"Who do I call first? Geraldo? Oprah? Newsweek? Time?"

"How do I get on the best-sellers list?"

"How do I advertise?"

My ego had lots of questions that I had no idea how to answer. The one thing I **did** know was that I was afraid. And so, instead of trying to get on the best seller list, what I committed to do was that every day I would take at least *one step* toward selling one of my books. That means that *anything* I did, even if it was just getting the phone number of a bookstore from the directory, counted. You see, I realized how scared I was of putting myself out into the world, but I knew that **any** step I took would count. It didn't matter if it was a big step or a small step. What mattered was going in the direction I wanted to go. Some days my fear of rejection was so great that all I could do was get a phone number or call one person. Other days, I would contact many sources.

I also began to listen and trust the support I got from others. I learned how to contact book distributors from a friend who had previously published his own material. Friends and clients knew bookstore owners and magazine editors to contact. I did not edit the ideas people gave me. I just listened and followed through, because I knew that at some level, God was supporting me through them. When I first published my book, I thought that I would succeed if I sold ten copies. The book is now in its fifth printing.

## *The Stages of Change*

In a seminar that Stav and I took from Joanne Tangedahl, LMSW, she presented a nice illustration that lists the four stages of how we change and grow. They are:

**Unconsciously Incompetent** - Our relationships do not work and we don't know why they don't work. We make the same mistake over and over. In short - we don't know that we don't know.

**Consciously Incompetent** - We may still make the same mistakes, but now we're beginning to see that we are the problem. We now know that we don't know.

**Consciously Competent** - We are getting better in relationships. It takes work and practice, but over time we improve. We are consciously working at getting competent.

**Unconsciously Competent** - The work we have done has now become second nature. We no longer have to actively remember how to be defenseless. We just are. We no longer have to actively practice listening to our partner. We just do. We unconsciously now do the right thing.

# Feeding Your Soul

I want to outline some of the steps Stav and I have taken in creating the kind of relationships that feed our souls.

*Have compassion for yourself and others.*

Treat yourself gently as you learn. When a baby is learning how to walk and it falls, it doesn't berate itself for being so stupid and clumsy. It cries, gets love and then stands up and tries again. Learning and growing in relationships is a constant process. We need to do it gently, cry when we fall, and then get up and do it again.

### Don't believe in initial appearances.

Remember that love *always* brings up everything unlike itself. Whenever you take a step into expanding your love and spirit, initially the situations in your life may actually look worse. Have you ever noticed that the day you decide to be more loving and accepting of others, that day it seems as if every idiot is on the street congregating around your car? Why is that? It's because as we claim we want to be more accepting, the Universe gives us a chance to practice it.

Whenever Stav and I are going to teach a workshop, we generally begin to process the workshop a week before it happens. If we're doing a Prosperity workshop, bills seem to crop up more than usual. If we're doing a Relationships workshop, we tend to get into more disagreements. If we're doing a Self-Esteem workshop, generally both of us feel down and unlovable. I won't tell you what happens when we teach a Sexuality workshop, but it's not fun!!!

But what Stav and I have learned is to not let the appearance of these problems stop us from giving a powerful workshop. We just keep taking our steps.

### Learn from the relationships you already have.

You don't need to be in an intimate relationship to learn. Do you realize that you are in a brief relationship with the sacker at your grocery store and that it is possible for him/her to feed your soul? Or are you blocking this experience? Are you shutting out the love?

When somebody gives you a compliment, it is an opportunity to let some love in and feed your soul. Do you let the love in, or do you block it? When your boss or lover praises you, do you let it in to feed your soul, or do you second guess their *real* reason for being so nice to you? Begin to see that maybe there are many daily opportunities to open to love.

### Forgive yourself—quick!

One of the best examples I've seen of this principle was at a Self Esteem workshop that was being taught by my friends Revs. Phil and Lura Smedstad. As Phil was going into his opening remarks, inviting the participants to let the day be an opportunity to learn to love and accept themselves at a deeper level, one of his students in the front row kept whispering something to him. He tried ignoring her, but kept getting distracted by her whispering. She kept motioning and whispering to him in a furtive manner. Finally, he couldn't take it any longer and he addressed her directly.

"What is it, Carol?"

Once again she mumbled something and motioned to him. Now Phil addressed the class.

"Carol here has been learning to claim her power and I think this is a great time for her to do so. Carol, tell us clearly and powerfully what you are trying to say!"

In a clear, powerful voice, she said, "Your pants are unzipped."

Phil zipped up, amid laughter (his own included), and remarked, "Well, I'm certainly glad this is not the Sexuality Workshop." He then took a breath, forgave himself quickly and continued to give a wonderful, inspired workshop.

When you take a step, any step, and you find that you did it wrong, forgive yourself and correct the error—quickly. It is not necessary to dwell on it any longer than it takes to find the correct answer. Then use that answer and move on.

### *Learn to take deep breaths often.*

"What!" you may say, "I breathe all the time!" Yes, but you may be breathing *just enough* to keep your body functioning, but not deeply enough to keep your life, your dreams, and your spirit alive. When a person begins to experience fear or any other negative feeling, the first thing that stops is the breath. The person naturally freezes and tightens up their body in a *fight or flight* stance in order to armor themselves against any perceived hurt. This response is useful when you are in physical danger, but we also react the same way when someone reprimands us, we get a traffic ticket, or our partner tells us something we don't want to hear. We shut down, raise our defenses and stop breathing, in an effort to not feel any pain.

Let me give you an example. Just the other day, I went to the dentist to have minor gum surgery. As he began working on me, I suddenly noticed how I wasn't breathing. I was actually holding my breath, terrified of anticipated pain. I've been doing breath work for over ten years and my body still reacts this way. What I did in that moment was to acknowledge the fear, soften my stomach and take slow, powerful breaths all the way down to the bottom of my lungs. After a few breaths, the fear lessened and I actually relaxed into the experience. And there was no pain or discomfort during or after the procedure.

When we don't relax our bodies and breathe through an experience, our bodies then literally store the memory of that experience in our cell tissue. Have you ever seen anybody who looks sad or angry—not only in their face, but in their body as well? By not breathing *through* an experience, we end up protecting ourselves from the momentary discomfort at the cost of storing that emotion and later feeling that discomfort *all the time*, drop by drop, moment by moment. We live life in suppressed fear, make decisions based on suppressed anger, try to love with suppressed love, and slowly are dying with suppressed life. When we do not allow ourselves to feel and release our negative feelings, we also don't allow ourselves to enjoy our positive feelings. Love is subdued. Compliments are not received. Sex becomes just an act -the pure enjoyment is lost.

A very effective way of opening our lives and relationships is a method of breathing called Breath Integration. It is a way of breathing in a circular way, never stopping the breathing cycle. There is no rest between breaths—the person is always inhaling or exhaling. As the body is flooded with oxygen on the inhale, and as it cleanses itself of toxins on the exhale, it begins to come alive. Thoughts or feelings that have been suppressed begin to rise to consciousness. This allows a person to face his/her fears, confront an old hurt or lay to rest an old issue. The body tingles with energy as the person opens up. Once the person faces and accepts his/her own issues, there is a sense of surrender and peace.

So just for a moment, put this book down and take ten deep, connected breaths—inhaling as deeply as you can and then exhaling as much as you can. Do you feel lightheaded? Is there a little tingling in your face? This is just a taste of the energy that is waiting within you to be used for good.

### See the world as a mirror of your own thoughts.

When you truly begin to realize that your thoughts create, you will begin to see that the world is always reflecting back to you your most inner, secret thoughts. Use this as a tool to better yourself. Is your partner always criticizing you? How do you criticize yourself? Do you complain because your partner does not love and acknowledge you? How do you withhold love from yourself and others? Every day try to take at least one aspect of the world that you do not like, and then take it inside, feel it and ask yourself, "What is the world trying to tell me about myself? In what way do I do the same thing? How can I correct this thought in me?" If you honor and correct only one thought a day, after a year you'll have corrected 365 thoughts. And **that** is progress!

### Write agreements.

The best time to work on a fight is before you hav/ when you are in your right minds and sane. Ask each o/ honor and respect when you are in disagreement about so'

Become aware of what pushes your buttons, and make conscious agreements around those topics. We all have certain words or actions that send us into rage or fear. Sit down with your partner and discuss what these hot items are, and then make agreements around alternative behaviors. If you know that storming from the room activates your partner's abandonment issues, you may be tempted to do it, just to hurt him/her, but try staying anyway. If storming from the room in self-righteousness is your defense against looking at issues that are uncomfortable, then know that staying in that room and facing those issues is the action that will lead to your own growth. That which you are *least inclined* to do is very often the very action that will stretch you and heal you the most!

When you are angry with each other, you will be tempted to break these agreements, but following them, even one out of ten times, is a 10% movement toward your sanity. And that, too, is progress!

### Seek counseling/mentoring to work on your own issues.

Does it seem as if I am continually trying to convince you to get into therapy? I am! Why? Because reading this or any other book, or doing workshops, plants the seeds of growth. But I have found (to paraphrase a legal quote) that when I try to counsel myself, I have a fool for a client. That is because I will be unable to see past any unconscious defenses I may have. If I read a section in a book that pertains to me, and I have resistance to acknowledging that it is true, I may find the book to be suddenly *very boring*. Or I may skip that section altogether. Or I may just tell myself,

"Boy I'm glad I don't have that going on with me! My wife does! But not me."

We all need a teacher, a mentor, a coach, to guide us. We need an objective observer to correct us when we err and lead us when we stray. There is a vast difference between knowledge and experience. Knowledge is what we get from workshops and books. Experience is what we get from applying and testing out what we have learned from workshops and books. There is a difference between reading about healing and actually healing. There is a vast difference between reading about heaven and actually going there.

If there are certain words or actions that throw you into rage and fear, get help in understanding and coping with these hot spots. Don't be afraid to go into the pain, because the peace and healing that result will far outweigh the pain.

For example, the word "fool" was my personal hot button. Whether the word was directed at me, mentioned in passing by an acquaintance, or even spoken in a movie, I would react. My spine would tingle, I would blush in anger and hurt, and I would feel like I wanted to either withdraw from the world or attack it. When I finally realized how I was affected and controlled by this word, I got help in feeling and releasing the emotions attached to that word. Breath Integration was the tool I found most effective in helping me to express and release my past, pent-up anger. As I began to realize the hold that word had over me, I became committed to releasing the hurt and pain associated with it.

To bring up even more feelings and healing, I actually went around, for awhile, saying to myself, over and over, "I am a fool, I am a fool, I am a fool." I continually let myself feel and acknowledge the hurt and rage this little word brought up in me. And I remembered to breathe as these feelings surfaced.

After about three days I suddenly found myself actually embracing the word and the feelings. "So what!" I said, the day it hit me, "Sometimes **I am** a fool. And sometimes I'm not! Everybody is at some time." The word had lost its power and no longer affects me. As Lao Tzu supposedly said, "The sage is a fool."

You can face your fears and monsters, but you don't have to do it alone. There are many more tools and techniques available that I have not covered in this book. There are many ways back to the love. Find the ways that work for you.

### *Every day do something to strengthen your relationship.*

Do you know how your partner likes to be loved? Do you know how *you* like to be loved? If you don't know how you like to be loved, how can your partner ever succeed in pleasing you? If you don't know how he/she wants to be loved, how can you ever win?

Make a list of how you like to be loved and share your lists with each other. Something I have loved about Stav is that early on in our relationship, she told me how she likes to be loved. I had spent years with women who expected me to be *Randi the Mindreader,* and it was refreshing to finally find someone who not only knew what she wanted, but also let me know.

So, make a list of all the ways that your partner can love you. Let them know how they can win with you. You may have items such as:

"Tell me you love me."

"Let others know you love me."

"Buy me flowers."

"Rub my feet."

"Leave little love notes around the house."

"Make the bed when I'm rushing to get ready for work."

And then every day do something from each other's list. My wife makes the bed every day. Personally, I *hate* making the bed, but every once in a while my Divine side prompts me to do it anyway, just because I love her. Once I remarked to her how much I disliked making the bed and she turned to me and said,

"And what makes you think *I* like making the bed?"

It occurred to me how many things my wife does that she does *not enjoy* but she does it anyway because she loves a tidy house, she loves herself and she loves me. It's her way of taking care of herself. In that moment I suddenly realized that I actually had the thought that women didn't mind cleaning the house, changing diapers, washing windows, writing thank-you notes and doing the dishes. It was as if I believed that they had some genetic predisposition toward cleaning.

I realized that day that keeping the house clean is not Stav's job alone. But if I won't do it, she'll take it on anyway. And so now I try to remember to make the bed, take out the garbage and generally tidy up, not just because I do like a nice house, but also to show that I appreciate and love her.

One night, at the end of one of my classes, I told the students to practice loving others the way they wanted to be loved. The following week a woman came up to me and told me that she tried my experiment. She decided to devote one day to each of her children, loving them the way they wanted to be loved. And so, she asked each child how he or she wanted to be loved on his or her day.

"I always thought I knew how to love my children best," she said, "but you know what? Each one wanted to be loved differently. The nine-year-old wanted to be loved with candy, so I bought him candy. The seventeen-year-old wanted me to love him by driving him around. Usually I tell him, 'Take the bus. You know how to use a bus schedule and tokens.'

"But on his day, I drove him around. The other two wanted to be loved with their favorite dinners and dessert. I still love my children in *my* way, but I learned a big lesson—to ask my children how they want to be loved in *their* way. And then I also do that."

How many times have we loved somebody the way *we thought* they wanted to be loved, and then became disappointed when the love wasn't received? How many times do we love somebody the way *we want to be loved* instead of how they want to be loved? The greatest gift we can give another is to stop loving them *our way* and to honor and respect them enough to hear their requests and then love them the way they want to be loved.

**Thank your partner, daily, for how he/she adds to your life.**
Something I also realized is that when I make the bed, I *expect* to be thanked for doing it. Stav does it every day and never gets thanks and yet when I do it once, I want her to notice. And you know what? She *does* notice it and thanks me for it. I now make it my job to notice

the things she does around the house and to let her know how much I appreciate her. And, most importantly, I try to help.

Too many times we take our partners for granted. We love and care about them, but many times get so caught up in our daily lives that we forget the people who are the most important to us. A good relationship is always growing and learning. There is a constant flow of love, loving words and loving deeds. These allow our roots to go deep and solid, able to withstand any of the storms that may challenge us.

### *If your relationship does not feed your soul, take responsibility.*

Stop blaming your partner for your state of life. It's time to begin to take stock of what is important to you, what feeds your soul and what drains you. And then you have to take responsibility to bring about the conditions that nurture and feed you. If you are in an abusive relationship, get help. Leave if you have to. Get out of the environment that is killing your spirit. It doesn't mean you have to get a divorce, but it does mean that you may need time to clear your head and decide what it is that you really want from this partnership.

### *Expand your horizons.*

Attend workshops and talk to couples who have the relationship you desire. Find new ways of relating and loving. At the end of this book is a suggested reading list of books that I have found to be helpful. Read them and apply the techniques that speak to you.

We have all seen the bumper sticker, "Visualize world peace." That is a wonderful and admirable statement. But I heard of a bumper sticker that goes one step further – "Forget world peace! Visualize using your turn signal!" It is easy to visualize world peace. The hard part is living that peace in our daily life.

Jack Kornfield, in his book, "*A Path With Heart*" says that at one point he realized he could practice "loving-kindness" meditations for *thousands of people* all over the world, but he could not be loving and kind to his immediate partner. Creating a relationship that feeds the soul requires that we become the type of person who can be fed and who can feed others.

So, visualize using your turn signals. Visualize trusting. Visualize setting boundaries. Visualize forgiving. Visualize a nurturing relationship. Visualize doing loving, caring things for yourself, your partner and others. Take those steps and make those visions real! And then stand back and watch how your life becomes sweeter, your partner becomes more loving towards you, and together, you reach new heights of love and joy.

## *Self Discovery Quiz*

- *Do my current relationships feed my soul? If not, what is missing? Is there something I can do or change within myself to change this situation?*

- *Do my relationships with others feed their souls?*

- *What is a step that I am secretly afraid of taking, but also I am secretly excited at taking?*

- *Do I take my relationship for granted? When is the last time I praised someone for who they are or how much they add to my life?*

- *Would I really die if I complimented my lover?*

- *Would I really die if I made the bed, took out the garbage or just cared about what my partner does?*

- *Are there new rules or agreements to be made concerning our relationship? How can we form a partnership that supports both of us?*

- *What is the worst that can happen if I take any step?*

- *What is the best that can happen if I take any step?*

*Make your words sweet –*
*in case you have to eat them!*

Rev. Ike

*The Bible tells us to love our neighbors,*
*and also to love our enemies;*
*probably because they are generally*
*the same people.*

G. K. Chesterton

*Swing hard, in case they happen to throw*
*the ball where you're swinging.*

Duke Snider

*Confidence, like art, never comes*
*from having all the answers;*
*it comes from being open*
*to all the questions.*

Earl Gary Stevens in *Home Education*

*The great secret of a successful marriage*
*is to treat all disasters as incidents*
*and none of the incidents as disasters.*

Harold Nicolson

# Getting Back to the Love . . .
## Even After a Fight

Nothing brings up opportunities for growth faster than a fight. This is where we test whether we are mature adults or squabbling children.

- In a healthy relationship, a fight **exposes lessons** to be learned. In an unhealthy relationship, a fight **exposes immaturity**.

- The goal of a fight in a healthy relationship is **resolution**. The goal of a fight in an unhealthy relationship is **victory**.

- A fight in a healthy relationship actually **strengthens** both people. A fight in an unhealthy relationship **tears down** and **weakens** each person.

I want to outline some steps a person can take when having an argument with another person. These are by no means the only steps to take, but use them as a starting point in transforming the old, unconscious relationships you have had to new, growing, conscious relationships. I have found that when I follow these steps, honoring myself and my partner along the way, I heal a lot faster. Now, after many, many arguments, most of these steps are instantaneous and take only minutes, whereas in the beginning sometimes it took as long as an hour (or a day, or a week) to be willing to change my mind enough to embrace a new idea.

You do not need to follow these steps in order. In fact, even if you pick a step at random, the *very act* of taking the step demonstrates that you want another way of looking at the problem. This in itself will slow you down and hopefully give your mind a chance to choose differently. This is a crucial step back into sanity—the willingness to change.

At first, when you begin to open up and share your truths, it may look like a big dump session. You may be too angry and do it wrong. But at least you took *a step*. Afterwards, look at the results. How long did it take to get back to loving each other? What went wrong? What did you do right? What areas need to be fine tuned? America did not send a man to the moon on its first try. It took years of mistakes, failures and lessons to finally create the technology that could do the job. You **will** learn how to be more responsible and defenseless through practice. Don't be afraid to ask for help, from God, from Jesus, from Buddha, from a counselor or a minister. It takes time and love. Give yourself a lot of both of them.

### Remember that both of you are 100% correct.

Are you willing to see that your partner truly believes that their view is correct? Are you willing to see that each of you has a very logical reason for thinking the way you do? Whether we are reacting to past hurts or imagined fears, in our minds they are real— in that moment. Allow yourself the thought, "My partner is **not** crazy for having this view. My partner is entitled to his/her view and I now honor it."

At any time, you can choose to escalate the argument or not. We have all experienced being at a point in an argument when we could *really* get the argument heated up, we could *really* hurt the other person with a well placed jab to their spirit, we could *really* get the other person jumping around like an idiot. And a part of us knows that that would be stupid. However, like fools, we jump into temptation, grab the opportunity and escalate the argument. We bring in old grudges and unforgiven items, we threaten, we call names. We attack their character or their family, just *because we are feeling a little threatened*.

Even though it may feel good for a moment, ask yourself, "Does it really pay to hurt or attack my partner more? Do I really want to continue this type of behavior when I am scared and defensive?"

If you are very tempted to escalate an argument, know that in that moment you are more interested in being right than in being happy. You are not yet ready to change your mind, nor are you open or willing to hear a different perspective. Instead of attacking, let your partner know that you are *not interested* in his or her side—*yet*. When you realize that *right now*, there is no way that you will change your mind, that you are not open to your partner's opinion, and that you are not willing to surrender and open up, at least both of you can stop beating your heads against each other's walls.

Acknowledging that you are not ready to see the other person's side is a powerful, conscious step on *your part* in claiming exactly what you want in the situation. Then, take time apart from each other. Notice how it feels to be alone. Notice how it feels to be right. And ask yourself, "How long do I want to be right? How long can I stew in this?" It has been my experience that after awhile, being a victim and pouting gets boring. When you notice that you're no longer getting as much enjoyment out of being right, then ask God for some help.

The important thing to remember is to be gentle with yourself and others *while you are insane*. Don't make the situation worse or unsolvable. It helps to remind yourself,

"I know these feelings will pass, and so I can be gentle with myself and my partner while I work out my feelings."

### Be willing to identify with the Observer.

Have you ever had an argument, and all the while that you are arguing, you can see both sides of your mind? There is the "Good" side that is urging you to be loving and understanding. And then there is the "Bad" side screaming for you to win this argument at all costs. The question I have for you is this:

If you can see both your Good and Bad side—**who is doing the looking?**

Be willing to step back from the argument into the role of the *Observer*. This *Observer* is your **True Mind**—the Decision Maker, the one that is always observing how you choose to heal or hurt. It doesn't judge you. It doesn't attack you. It just watches, knowing all the time what will really bring you happiness. Ask this Observer what to do. It will always answer in a way that will bring you more peace. It is the Christ, Holy Spirit, Buddha, God in you.

### Take responsibility for how you feel right now.

If you need to, take time out to pout, run off your victim thoughts, and even blame—**privately**—but do not openly attack the other person with blame or projection. This only increases guilt and defensiveness. When I get angry with Stav and I want to be right, I know that there is no way that she can get through to me. And so I take a long, brisk walk and stew in my anger and hurt, or I just sit and stew. I allow myself the *luxury* of being a victim and blaming her for all of my problems. I wallow in my grievances. Usually, after a few minutes (or hours, sometimes), I get tired of being right and miserable. Then I am more *willing* to hear her side.

### Check in and see how your body feels.

Sometimes we may not be aware of all of the feelings involved in an issue. We can deny our emotions, but our bodies never lie. Our bodies merely mirror what is going on inside our minds. Is your breathing shallow and tight? Are your muscles sore? Does your back, neck, or arms hurt? If you notice any kind of discomfort, instead of resisting it, surrender to it. *Allow* yourself to experience the pain and tightness.

Even though I have done years of work on myself, there are still times when I experience pain from an old, old hurt and just by allowing it to surface, I begin to heal. As you allow the discomfort to just *be*, you may feel old sorrow or anger or abandonment that you never realized was there. So many times we get into arguments, never realizing that what we may be fighting is the fear of a repetition of an old hurt. We fear being left again or laughed at again and we strike out, never seeing how a past issue is affecting the current situation.

### Ask yourself, "What is my intention around this issue?"

Do you want to learn about yourself and grow? Or do you want to protect, defend and blame? Is your intention to *win* the argument at all costs? Or is it to come to an agreement that both of you feel good about? What is your purpose in your relationship? Love? Or always winning?

If your original intention is different from what you are currently creating, ask yourself, "Where did I get off track with my intention?"

Many times our intentions may be to help, but the other person may not be in a position to hear our support. Or maybe what you thought your intention was, was not what you *really* intended. Sometimes when we help with *good intentions*, we may not be aware that our egos are also driving our intentions. A desire to help may actually be a mask to make us feel better by covering our own low self esteem.

When I am not getting the results I expect (ie: my purpose is to love and support), but instead my partner is getting angry and defensive, I have found it is helpful to question my deeper intentions to see whether I had another secret goal.

### Be willing to let go of your pride.

Remember that relationships are for healing, and as we heal, we will see sides of ourselves of which we are not proud. If you realize during the course of an argument that you have been wrong (this *has* been known to happen—even to me), take a deep breath, let yourself be defenseless—and apologize. Acknowledge your mistake and get back to loving each other.

### Breathe, Breathe, Breathe!

When you notice that you are defensive or in fear, let your stomach muscles relax so that you can take deep breaths all the way down to the bottom of your lungs. When we are angry, we armor our bodies with tight muscles, shallow breathing and preparedness for fight or flight. If the anger is very intense, scream into a pillow or hit a bed with a tennis racket to help release the pent-up feelings.

Venting the toxic feelings appropriately is a lot more empowering, and much safer, than destroying the relationship with destructive acts or words. As you are expressing these feelings, take deep powerful breaths into your lungs. In this way, you will more quickly embrace the anger and fear, and as you breathe into it, the feeling will gradually dissipate.

### Remember that all anger is actually a fear of loss.

When you are angry, ask yourself, *"What am I afraid of losing right now?"* Many times, after having a long, drawn-out argument, Stav and I will realize that what was really going on is that we were afraid— afraid of losing control, love, money, self esteem or anything else.

If we notice ourselves during an argument, we will see that frequently we act like two year-olds. We need to acknowledge and love those children inside us and remind them that they will not lose, that we will love and protect them. I also find that an argument quickly gets defused when the participants begin to share their fears about what they *think* the other person has done to them. They soon realize that they both have the same fears. This actually builds a bridge between the two. Now instead of arguing about differences, they are working together to alleviate their fears—together.

I had a couple, Kate and Greg, who were seeing me for counseling concerning a move to Colorado. This move entailed not only a change of home but also the sale of the husband's business—a business he had built from scratch. Needless to say, there were a lot of feelings to be expressed.

One of their issues concerned the fact that since they were

planning to relocate, Greg felt they should not be spending any money unless absolutely necessary. Kate, on the other hand, seemed to ignore his desires and would continue to spend as she always had. She would buy clothing for the cold weather and toys for the children. In fact, it seemed to Greg that she was spending more.

They would fight and accuse each other of control and manipulation. He would argue that he was only trying to help them attain a dream that they both had wanted, but she wasn't helping. She would feel guilty, but then defend herself by pointing out that these were items they would need anyway, and besides, was the family supposed to stop spending money indefinitely? It looked like a stalemate.

When I supported them to share their separate fears, a different side emerged. He shared that he was afraid that since he was selling his business and attempting to start all over in a new state, they wouldn't have enough money. He was only trying to conserve what they already had. He was afraid that there wouldn't be enough money.

She had similar fears, but handled them with a different method. Since she feared that there wouldn't be enough money *later*, she was spending the money *now*, while they had some. She was buying the coats and the toys because later they wouldn't be able to afford them. She also was afraid that there wouldn't be enough money.

When they saw that they had the same fear, but just different ways of handling it, they visibly relaxed. Suddenly they no longer saw each other as the enemy. Now they had a *common problem*. From this standpoint, they then began to discuss how they could share their fears and support each other through the fears.

### Be willing to see this situation through God's eyes.

Step back and ask yourself, *"What would Jesus (or Buddha, or Mohammed, or Confucius, or...) say or do in this situation? How would He/She see what is going on? Am I missing any facts that need to be seen?"* When you ask yourself to see the situation through God's eyes, it will give you a different perception. You may have thoughts like, *"Will this issue even matter a day, a week or a hundred years from now?"*

A woman in one of my classes related a wonderful experience she had in seeing a situation through different eyes. She told us,

"There was this very beautiful woman who 23 years ago tried to seduce my husband (We have since divorced). She made a very concerted effort to get him. And my husband was so naïve that he actually asked me if he could have an affair with her. Of course I told him 'Hell, no!'"

"Anyway, she called me up a few weeks ago and asked me to come do some work for her. I could not *believe* she had the **audacity** to call me and ask for my services! I was in a state of shocked disbelief and I initially thought, 'This *really* couldn't be her' and so I put her off and told her I was on the other line and would get back to her later."

"I called a couple of friends and they basically said, '*Build a bridge and get over it. This could be an experience of a lifetime.*' And so I decided to listen to them and for about three hours I was physically sick, literally, with vomiting and nausea. I kept replaying what I felt. The betrayal. The sneakiness. The underhandedness. The audacity and all of that. Then I called her back and made the appointment to see her. And then, just before I got there I finally decided that NO WAY could this be the same woman."

"Well, it *was* her."

"But in the process of meeting with her, I also got to meet her husband. What I experienced was that the man that she's married to now looks *exactly* as my ex-husband would have looked at this age. And I suddenly got that there was no way that she couldn't but be attracted to my ex-husband at the time. Where I thought there might have been some malice or 'How could she do that!', I realized that she couldn't help herself. She's clearly attracted to that kind of man!"

"And I thought 'Oh! She had no malice for me. She was not out to get me. She just liked him! That's all. She *really* liked him! No big deal! He just *happened* to be my husband.'"

"And so I'm doing this job for her and I'm doing one of the finest jobs I've ever done. If I had wanted to hold onto what a bitch I thought she was, I would still be stuck with all those old feelings and beliefs."

I consider her one of the lucky ones. Though it took 23 years, she finally had an opportunity to see a situation with new eyes. Now, ask yourself, can I possibly speed up my own process, so that I can see my situation with new eyes in maybe ten years, five years, one month, one week, one day or maybe even a minute from now?

### *Whoever gets sane first—call someone for support.*

Get an objective opinion from somebody who believes in your innocence. Do not get support from people who do not support your highest good (i.e.: buddies at the bar, gossip groups, pity pals, etc.). True support can be a counselor, sponsor, minister or just a friend that you trust. If you know of somebody whose relationship works, who demonstrates integrity in their life, and who will tell you the truth, call them. And remember to be defenseless as you talk to them.

### *Take turns telling your truth—without interruption.*

Another method of communication was covered in the chapter on Defenselessness, but this topic cannot be emphasized enough! Here I am covering another variation of Defenseless Listening.

Decide who will talk first (sender) and who will listen (receiver). The agreement here is that when one person is finished talking, the other person will then talk while their partner listens, without interrupting. *Do not break this agreement.* You need to develop trust in your relationship, and this is one action that is sorely needed. Remember, listen without thinking or planning your reply. Just listen. Nothing else.

The only thing that the listener is allowed to say is to reflect back to the sender what he/she just said. You can do this after every few sentences or after the speaker is finished talking. If what the listener repeats back is not correct, the sender merely corrects it until the listener hears it right. This insures that the correct message was given and received. The purpose of listening and responding this way is to increase communication. Many times what is heard is **not** what was said. For example,

"Jerry, I get upset when you work late and you don't call me and let me know."

"So you don't want me working late at the office anymore!" (This is a typical defensive response.)

"No, Jerry, that's not what I said. I get worried when you are late. I want you to call when you are late."

"So if I understand you, Stav, you get afraid when I am late and you want me to call you. It's not about me working late, it's about letting you know."

"That's right."

Then proceed to the next message. Also, let God, the Holy Spirit or Jesus speak for you. Many times, when I cannot verbalize what is going on, I find that letting them do the talking gets me in touch more quickly with the real issue.

Once the sender is done sharing his/her side, there are two very good tools you can use to complete the process: Validate and then Empathize with your partner. These tools were formulated by Harville Hendrix, the author of *Getting the Love You Want* and founder of Imago Therapy. Here's how they work..

First, the receiver validates the sender.

"This makes sense. I see that you get afraid when I do not come home on time, and you want to know that I am safe. Actually, I would want the same thing from you." (*Validate*)

"That's right."

"And I imagine you must feel scared, anxious and probably a little angry." (*Empathize*)

"Yes I do."

Validating and empathizing allows the receiver to see that the sender is not crazy—that there are *valid reasons* for their beliefs and feelings. You still do not have to agree with your partner, but hopefully you understand them a little more.

When the sender is done, give yourselves a few moments to breathe and assimilate what you have shared. Then switch roles and tell your side, repeating the same process.

### Ask for a win-win.

Ask God to show you how both of you can be happy with an outcome. Remember, as soon as you ask for a win-win, your powerful minds will begin to search for the answer. Give yourselves time to surrender to God's love and wisdom. If you have a hard time believing that there is an answer to your problem, ask yourself, *"Is God big enough to solve this or is my problem bigger than God?"* It also helps to tell your partner that you **do** want him/her to win and that **you also** want to win. And it helps if your partner tells you the same thing.

### If you say mean, hurtful things, ask for forgiveness.

When you are wrong, apologize. Take responsibility for *your* behavior. Don't justify your behavior based on what they did. Take full responsibility for your attacks. The saying, "Two wrongs do not make a right," has always been true and always will be. If you are wrong, admit it and get on with healing your relationship.

### Make it easy for the other person to apologize.

Do you know those times when both of you are angry with each other and, after awhile, you want to stop fighting? How do you initiate reconciling? How do you extend your feelers to see if it's safe? Do you remark about the weather? Or is it just small talk—your way of trying to break the ice—that really says "I am ready to connect now?" Do you know what your partner's signs are when he/she is ready to open up? If you don't know, ask him/her.

Everybody fights, and everybody shuts down and withdraws. This is part of our defenses. But we need to know when it is time to open up, and we need to make it easy for the other person to do so also. Refrain from remarks such as: "I told you so," and "If only you'd listen!" If your partner apologizes, be willing to forgive him/her. It takes a lot of courage and self-esteem to be willing to reconcile or to admit you are wrong. Acknowledge that courage in yourself and your partner.

### *Be willing to laugh - Remember how you started.*

As I stated earlier, laughter can defuse any situation. I have two friends, Jack and Claire, who told me about a wonderful incident in their marriage.

One night, Jack was out late entertaining clients. Though Claire did not mind him taking clients out, she didn't like when Jack stayed out too late. This particular night, as it got later and later, Claire began to get angrier and angrier. Finally around 12:30 she collected her blanket from their bed and self-righteously moved to the guest bedroom, where she slept fitfully.

Around 3:00 she woke up to go to the bathroom and then decided to return to their room. Jack was home, snoozing away. Claire was still angry and was debating what action to take when she suddenly saw something on her pillow. Looking closer she saw that it was a baby picture of Jack. She told me,

"There was no way I could stay angry with him! That image of that little innocent boy wrecked my mood!"

Last week Jack and Claire celebrated their fiftieth anniversary.

When you are angry with each other, be willing to remember the reasons you got into a relationship in the first place. Remember what initially attracted you to each other. And take yourselves, and your problems, lightly.

### *Give yourselves time to heal.*

Sometimes after a fight, the stormy seas in our hearts need time to settle down. Take some quiet time, either together or apart, but in silence, to help you to integrate what transpired. If you choose, you can hold each other, again in silence. Don't try to figure out everything that was going on in the argument. Most likely, you will have ideas and revelations in the following days.

Remember that you are human and you will make mistakes.

Do not expect to always *do relationships right*. Even after years of training, you will still find yourself tempted to go back to your old patterns, but do not let this deter you. The cruelest thing we can do to ourselves is to not allow ourselves to make mistakes.

At times, you will forget to apply these steps. At times you will be more interested in winning or being right. So what! Forgive yourself! Forgive yourself! Forgive yourself! And, when all else fails, forgive yourself again!

---

# *Affirmations*

- *I am always committed to getting back to the love in my relationship.*

- *Whenever I am challenged, my spirit rejoices in another opportunity to grow.*

- *I now allow my partner to help me to heal and grow.*

- *Whenever I am upset, I know that I do not have all the facts.*

- *Nobody can upset me unless I am already upset. I am now willing to see my part in any disagreement.*

- *An argument can make me feel closer or further apart from my partner. I now choose closeness.*

- *No matter what I have to do, I now claim more love in my life.*

*Oh God, help me to believe the truth about
myself no matter how beautiful it is.*

Macrina Wiederkehr, *Seasons of Your Heart*

*Everybody brightens up a room,
some by entering it, some by leaving.*

**Anonymous**

*I could not say I believe.
I know!
I have had the experience
of being gripped by something
that is stronger than myself,
something that people call God.*

**Carl Jung**

*The Christian ideal has not been tried
and found wanting.
It has been found difficult,
and left untried.*

**C. K. Chesterton**

# In Conclusion

Relationships can be fun! That is ultimately their true purpose—that as we heal, we remember who we really are (children of God), and we open up and enjoy life!

Whether we think we deserve it or not, we are all destined to be happy. It is only a matter of time. As the *Course* says, we do not have a choice in whether or not we will experience heaven. The only choice we have is *when*.

Everything in this book is designed to help shorten that time it takes us to change our minds enough to want to experience heaven. Remember that relationships have a physical and spiritual nature, and remember to honor both. Open to the love that started in your relationships, and learn how to keep the fires burning.

Having relationships that are alive, empowering and fun is part of the joy of being a human being. It is the discovery of the love that is all around us and within us that makes our lives worth living.

Don't be afraid to take new steps. But even if you are afraid, take those steps anyway. The truth about you is not limited to the world you see. Begin to open your inner eyes, begin to open your heart and mind to new ideas. When you do, you will experience the truth about yourself.

You may have noticed the butterflies in this book. I hope the analogy is obvious. It represents transformation. Deep within every caterpillar is the knowledge of what it will be. When that knowledge is activated, beautiful and stunning changes occur. So too, with our relationships. Within each of us is the knowledge of what is possible and what we can become. Transform yourself and your relationships and once again learn to fly.

# Comes the Dawn
## by Veronica A. Shoffstall

After awhile you learn the subtle difference between
holding a hand and chaining a soul
And you learn that love doesn't mean possession
and company doesn't mean security.

And you begin to learn that kisses aren't contracts
and presents aren't promises and you begin to accept
your defeats with your head up and your eyes ahead
with the grace of an adult not the grief of a child.

And you learn to build your roads today because
tomorrow's ground is too uncertain for plans and
futures have ways of falling down in mid-flight.

After awhile you learn that even sunshine
burns if you get too much so you plant your
own garden and decorate your own soul
instead of waiting for someone to bring you flowers.

And you learn that you really can endure
that you really are strong
and you really have worth
and you learn
and you learn . . .

# How to Use Affirmations

(Reprinted from *Compassionate Living - Everyday Spirituality*)

Affirmations have been an important tool in changing my life. Since we create with our minds, it is important to retrain our minds out of old, negative, self-sabotaging beliefs to beliefs that support a loving, abundant lifestyle. I have seen my life change dramatically from lack and struggle with relationships, to increased prosperity, loving, harmonious relationships and a greater sense of peace in my world. As the saying goes, "A mind is a terrible thing to waste." Let's use this powerful tool, not miscreate with it.

Some of the techniques I use are:

- Use your name when writing affirmations. This gets the attention of the mind easier. If you are doing work around your childhood or with your inner child, use the name you were called as a child. If you had a nickname, use that also.

- Repeat the affirmation throughout the day to constantly remind yourself of the new thought you want to embrace. Repeat to yourself the new thought on the way to work. Instead of cursing the traffic, repeat the affirmations. Saying them out loud also utilizes your ears. I also find that saying them in different voices (loud, soft, whisper, silly) enhances the introduction of the new idea.

- Writing the affirmation multiplies the benefit because it uses more of the body's senses. Remember, the more of the body's senses that can be marshaled in your change, the quicker the message sinks in. Write the affirmation in the three tenses, or persons, five to ten times per day. For example,

| | |
|---|---|
| *I, Jerry, now accept myself.* | *(5 - 10 times)* |
| *You, Jerry, now accept yourself.* | *(5 - 10 times)* |
| *Jerry now accepts himself.* | *(5 - 10 times)* |

- Write the affirmations for at least a week.

- To see how your mind responds to these new ideas, you can write a response for each line you write. To do this, draw a line vertically on the page about one-third of the way from the right edge. This will be your "response column." When you finish writing a line of affirmation, write the **first** thought that pops into your mind. For example,

| | |
|---|---|
| *I, Jerry, now accept myself.* | What a lie! |
| *I, Jerry, now accept myself.* | I hate this! |
| *I, Jerry, now accept myself.* | I'm willing. |

When writing your response, don't edit your thoughts. Just write them as they are. Over time you can see how your resistance to the new idea is changing. When you get to a place where you notice no particular thought around an affirmation, neither good nor bad, know that the new thought has now been accepted into your thought system.

- Create a cassette tape with your affirmations on it. It is interesting and wonderful to hear your own voice telling you new thoughts about yourself, affirming the truth about who you are. You can then play it on the way to work, before sleeping or any other time. Use a five or ten minute "endless loop" cassette tape available at stores like Radio Shack.

- Don't be afraid to create your own affirmations. Look at the areas in your life that need change and start affirming what it is you desire in each situation. Do you want more peaceful relationships? Affirm that. Do you want increased prosperity? Affirm that. Look at the thoughts that are causing problems in your life and turn them around into positive, life affirming statements. If you think that there is never enough money, create an affirmation like, "I now know that there is more than enough time, love and money for me." If you have trouble coming up with ideas, ask your lover, your friends, your minister for help.

• Also begin to look around in your life where you may be creating **negative** affirmations. What do you think bumper stickers such as "Shit Happens!" affirm? I have a friend who was always complaining about her lack of money. One day I noticed something that she had printed on her checks—"Money talks. Mine says good-bye." When I pointed this out, she quickly ordered a new set of checks and tossed the old ones out. On our checks, Stav and I have printed, "God is the source of our abundance." This helps to remind us and anyone who sees our checks that it is God, not our job or clients, who is the source of all our good.

As the affirmations begin to work, one of two things will happen:

The situation will improve,

**OR**

The situation will appear to get worse

In either case, *do not* stop the affirmations. When things get better, we tend to think the work is done, and then we stop, never realizing that the affirmation still needs a little more work to get inside. Continuing with the affirmation for another week cements the foundation you worked so hard to establish.

When things appear to get worse, remember that this, too, is *temporary*. As you work on expanding the Divine truth within you, it will push to the surface every unloving thought. As you become aware of these old thoughts, you can release them, but first you must become aware of them. This is the time to persevere. Continue the affirmations **no matter what,** until you see a change. You *will* see a change because life is your tool, not your master.

Since affirmations bring to our consciousness any suppressed thoughts, they also bring up the feelings that are associated with those thoughts. Old thoughts that we are stupid, worthless and sleazy have charged emotions attached to them. It is not uncommon to feel sad, depressed or angry during this time. This, too, is temporary. The feelings will pass as you reaffirm these new beliefs and begin experiencing a change in your outer world.

Learning about yourself is not a solitary process so, if possible, develop a support system. People who understand what you are going through can help immensely. Counselors, ministers, friends and support groups have been invaluable in my growth process. Many times, I needed to hear a word of encouragement from somebody who experienced similar things, or at least from someone who didn't believe in my littleness. As you grow, others will grow with you, and you can grow from their experience.

And remember, **you cannot do it wrong.** When you have the intention to heal yourself—you will! So use the affirmations in this book, or other books, or make up your own. God loves you, and where there is a desire to go home, He will help.

# Suggested Reading

*A Course in Miracles.* Need I say anything more? If you feel drawn to it, study it. If you get lost, find a study group to help. Every city has at least one group to help.

*Compassionate Living - Everyday Spirituality* by Rev. Jerome Stefaniak. This is a great book about learning to have compassion for yourself, no matter what. It is a candid look at the process of growing spiritually and emotionally as you live an everyday life. Written by my favorite author, me, it draws on my personal experience of learning to love and appreciate myself, life and others.

*A Return to Love* by Marianne Williamson. This book has helped introduce *A Course in Miracles* to millions of people. Ms. Williamson does an excellent job of explaining the concepts of the *Course* as they relate to relationships.

*Forgiveness and Jesus* by Ken Wapnick. If you are going to be in a relationship, you will be given many opportunities to forgive. Ken Wapnick was one of the first people who were introduced to the *Course*. He explains what forgiveness is and the benefits of it.

*A Path with Heart* by Jack Kornfield. I love this book! Mr. Kornfield spent eight years in Thailand, learning Eastern philosophy, meditation and other disciplines for the purpose of bringing order into his life. When he came home to New York, he then found that all of his problems he thought he had left behind were still waiting for him. He realized then that part of the purpose of his spiritual pursuits had been to run away from his problems. This book is a candid, in-depth approach to spirituality that isn't afraid to address our emotions or the issues that confront us.

*Conscious Loving* by Gay and Kathryn Hendricks. Using Conscious Breathing as a technique, Gay and Kathryn take the reader through the pitfalls of relationships and the personal resistance one finds in accepting oneself. They help the reader to understand how we are the problem, and that the problem can really be corrected. I personally love their concept of the "Upper limits" problem, which states that when we reach a point of too much good in our life, we will find a way to diminish it. When our relationship is too stable and happy, we'll find a way to rock the boat.

*Two Hearts are Better than One* and *Open Heart Therapy* by Bob Mandel. Both of these books address many of the issues regarding our feelings. He does a great job of explaining the importance of recognizing the feelings that we have, why we have them, and how to release any negative feelings and thoughts. He also explains the Rebirthing Principle of deep breathing and release.

*Opening Our Hearts to Men* by Susan Jeffers. Ms. Jeffers takes on the attitude that the problem with our relationships is not the other person, it's our inability to let the other person in. She takes the reader on an inner journey through his/her judgements and fears around opening to men. Though written for women, the exercises and examples apply wonderfully in showing us how to open up more to another person, whether male or female.

*Women Who Run with the Wolves* by Clarissa Pinkola Estes, Ph.D. This book is not only for women! The stories and examples, though geared toward women, are universal and very powerful. I easily related to many of the issues, such as losing one's power, the fear of change and suppressed sexuality. Ms. Estes is a great storyteller and interpreter! Her explanation of the story of *Skeleton Women* is a powerful primer on how relationships evolve.

*Getting the Love You Want* by Harville Hendrix, Ph.D. Dr. Hendrix was one of the first speakers I heard who actually sees relationships as a path to healing and wholeness. He also uses his personal experiences to illustrate a point and to remind the reader that he, too, used to struggle with relationships. His tapes, books and presentations are warm, witty and insightful.

*Facing the Fire* by Bill Stott. If you have a problem with anger, this is the book for you. Mr. Stott helps the reader to look at, acknowledge and then deal with this powerful and mostly misunderstood emotion.

*Anatomy of the Spirit* by Caroline Myss. I love what Caroline Myss teaches. She has integrated the Eastern teachings of the energy systems (chakras) with Western religion and philosophy. She has an obvious love of God that comes through her talks and writings. Her tapes are particularly powerful. Don't be surprised if she ruffles your feathers. I have found many of the things she says to be initially disturbing, but then, upon reflection, very true. I find her to be very wise and extremely grounded.

# The Most Fun You'll Ever Have Learning About Love, Life and Yourself!

- Does life really have to be hard?
- Are we doomed to continually keep making the same mistakes, over and over, without relief?
- Is it possible to finally feel a sense of peace with oneself? To actually feel love and compassion for who we are?
- Do we have to first be perfect before we are worthy to be loved?

*Compassionate Living - Everyday Spirituality* by Jerome Stefaniak is a warm, wonderful book that is helping people change how they see themselves and life. It is a practical guide to living a spiritual life in a very material and human world. Based on the teachings of *A Course in Miracles*, this book is for anyone who seeks a spiritual path but still wants to be able to relate to the everyday world.

In fact, not since Marianne Williamson has a writer so skillfully brought to life the principles of *A Course in Miracles*, relating them to daily living in the real world. But it doesn't matter if one is a student of the *Course* or not; the message in *Compassionate Living* is universal. Distilled to its purest essence, the book is about self-love, self-acceptance and self-healing. The powerful stories, explanations, questions and affirmations slowly guide the reader to an awareness that it is possible to love and accept oneself right now. And that the journey can be fun and humorous!

For those who thought spirituality and practicality were mutually exclusive, this book will be an eye-opener. For those who never had any doubt that the two could happily co-exist, Jerry Stefaniak's book is a joyous affirmation.

*This is the most personally revealing, down-to-earth, and absolute funniest journey to self-awareness and love that I have ever read. It is one book I found myself not wanting to put down. It's sure to become a self-help, spiritual* **hit**.
**Annah Mesko, Book Reviewer for the Houston Indigo Sun**

*Reading "Compassionate Living - Everyday Spirituality" was delightful as well as powerful. It was like having a conversation with a wise and witty friend. We joyfully recommend that you read it.* **The Reverends Phil and Lura Smedstad**

*You have created a splendid book. It is full of sound principles which are presented in an original manner. I found your personal anecdotes moving; in fact several of them made me cry. Your book touched me.* **Connie Schmidt, Editorial Consultant**

*I couldn't put your book down. I enjoyed every page. It is easy to read and full of wisdom. It will assist me in getting to where I'd like to be. Thank you for a great book!*
**Richard Humphrey - Leasing Specialist**

*My favorite part of the book is your honesty woven into every chapter. I loved the depiction of your fight with your wife, culminating in the realization that sometimes we just want to be mad and have no desire to be convinced of our lovability. I can relate to that. Your book inspires truth-telling. It is refreshing to hear someone come clean with their feelings. You are a great teacher of love.* **Mysti Lee Rudd, Spiritual Teacher**

Title: *Compassionate Living — Everyday Spirituality*
Author: Jerome Stefaniak
ISBN: 0-9638758-3-3                    Retail Price: $14.95

# A Course in Miracles Overview

If you are interested in learning more about *A Course in Miracles*, there is no better way of understanding the con cepts than by attending Jerry Stefaniak's classes. The next best thing is listening to his tapes. His six tape overview series on *A Course in Miracles* is an excellent resource for new and seasoned students of the *Course*. It covers the basic concepts of the *Course*, how it applies to your life, and practical support in using these ideas in your daily life. This series also includes his wonderful meditations.

Reverend Stefaniak uses humor, real down-to-earth, day-to-day examples and his own life to help the listener understand these wonderful and powerful lessons. Altogether, the tapes total about **nine hours** of spiritual and practical support. The topics covered are:

- *What Are Miracles?*
- *What Is the Ego?*
- *Love and Fear*
- *Releasing Judgements*
- *Creating Healthy Relationships*
- *Forgiveness*

---

If you would like to have Jerry speak at your organization about personal transformation or would simply like to comment on ***Intimacy in Action - Relationships that Feed the Soul***, please forward your correspondence to:

Reverend Jerome Stefaniak

Inner Awakenings

11306 Overbrook, Houston TX 77077

(713) 785-3131

After graduating from the University of Illinois with a BS in Accounting, Jerry took his graduate work at De Paul University, earning an MBA in Systems Analysis in 1978. During that time and for the following seven years, he successfully pursued a career in business computing.

In 1985 Jerry began a program of personal development which in 1986 led him into a new career: sharing with others the principles and techniques he had successfully learned to apply in his own life.

An accomplished speaker, Jerry has delivered numerous speeches and meditations to various clubs, churches and organizations in various states. He leads classes in *A Course in Miracles* at Unity Church of Christianity in Houston, TX. As a spiritual teacher, Jerry offers private consultations for individuals and couples, using Breathwork to unblock and release suppressed thoughts and emotions.

Along with his wife, Stavroula (Stav), they teach public workshops, intensive Six-Month Personal Development Programs and professional trainings for Breath Integration practitioners. They are the founders of Inner Awakenings, a company dedicated to the spiritual growth and personal transformation of individuals.

He is also author of the well-received book, *Compassionate Living - Everyday Spirituality.*

Stav Stefaniak, LMSW-ACP, is a state-licensed psychotherapist and Breath Integration practitioner and is in private practice in Houston, TX. Stav has over 25 years experience in the mental health field. She developed and presented numerous workshops, spoke at national conventions and co-authored published articles.